the professional's guide to
<mark>mining</mark> the internet

2nd edition

the professional's guide to
`mining` the internet

2nd edition

information gathering and research on the net

brian clegg

To Philip Mudd for saying 'If you could just write...'.

First published 1999

Second edition 2001

Apart from any fair dealing for the purposes of research or private study, or criticism or review, as permitted under the Copyright, Designs and Patents Act 1988, this publication may only be reproduced, stored or transmitted, in any form or by any means, with the prior permission in writing of the publishers, or in the case of reprographic reproduction in accordance with the terms and licences issued by the CLA. Enquiries concerning reproduction outside these terms should be sent to the publishers at the undermentioned addresses:

Kogan Page Limited
120 Pentonville Road
London
N1 9JN
UK

Stylus Publishing Inc.
22883 Quicksilver Drive
Sterling
VA 20166-2012
USA

© Brian Clegg, 1999, 2001

British Library Cataloguing in Publication Data

A CIP record for this book is available from the British Library.

ISBN 0 7494 3655 7

Typeset by Saxon Graphics Ltd, Derby
Printed and bound in Great Britain by Clays Ltd, St Ives plc

Contents

Preface

When *Mining the Internet* first came out in 1999, the Internet already contained a vast, confusing mix of incredibly useful information and garbage. Since then, the volume of information has exploded. The good news about using the Internet for research is that almost anything you want to know is probably out there somewhere. The bad news is that it is like searching for a particular item on a bulletin board, planted with millions of other boards in a field the size of Texas.

In the new edition of this book we reflect the changes since 1999 – the breadth of information sources, the new wave of e-commerce, the changing vehicles for getting to the Net – but the main purpose of the book continues to be to take the pain out of using the Internet as an information source, whether you need to know what's on at your local theatre, to find a telephone number of a company on the other side of the world, or to produce in-depth research material for your academic studies. It provides simple, practical ways to improve your ability to find the right information, with specific application-focussed sections to chase up specific requirements.

The Internet is much too fluid for a guidebook to provide more than a taster. Instead of taking the user on a tour of the Internet, this book builds the skills needed to be your own explorer. It keeps the subject light, concentrating on the information rather than the technology. The book is split into skills chapters, building your expertise on finding things on the Internet, and focus chapters, looking at particular information topics.

Mining the Internet is a shortcut to becoming an expert Internet navigator. Using a combination of readable text and handy side references, it will give you the guidance you need to tame the Internet. This is the book you'll want to keep beside your PC.

1 SKILLS

1 *It's out there somewhere*

- How this book will help;
- Exploring what the Internet (and the Web) is, and equally importantly what it isn't;
- Jumping to particular pages to deal with an urgent requirement.

WHY MINE THE INTERNET?

We all need information. Whether you need to find out what's on at the local multiplex or research the life cycle of the sandfly, information is the oil of civilization. Once upon a time, this meant using a whole raft of sources. The local paper, an encyclopedia, a library – now we've got the biggest source ever, wired straight into everyone's home: the Internet. (Okay, it might not be wired into your home yet – if so, see the Appendix on getting connected.)

WHY USE THIS BOOK?

It's not plain sailing. You can't throw away your library cards yet. The Internet has its limitations. But forget those merchants of doom who moan that the Internet is just an unfathomable mess – with the right approach, it is still streets ahead of anything else ordinary mortals have access to. You do need the right approach, though, and that's what this book is here to give you. It's a course in toning up your inquisitiveness, putting some gloss on the mental muscles to help you to find what you need. The chapters are divided into two types – skills chapters (like this one) give you plenty of information and are more designed to read straight through. Focus chapters (7 to 10) look at very specific information you can get from the Web. Because of this there are more examples and less general help.

There are various boxes scattered around the text, which fall into four neat categories. *Zoom in* boxes provide a little extra detail on a particular subject. If it interests you, plunge in. If it doesn't, feel free to ignore it (though you will be missing out). *Try it* boxes are practical exercises to do right now. Your ability to navigate the Internet will improve with practice – so get some. *Sample sites* boxes highlight real Web sites or newsgroups that you might want to visit: they don't provide a definitive list, just a sample to act as a taster. As the Web is the most fluid of environments, some of these addresses will be out-of-date before you get to try them – mostly, though, I've stuck to long-term hopefuls – sites which will probably be around for a fair while. The last type of box, *miners' tales*, gives real-life examples of whatever is being discussed.

Sample Sites

Mining the Internet updates

Here's the first box, just to get the hang of them. If you find any of the references in *Mining the Internet* are out-of-date, or just want to exchange comments, drop me an e-mail at brian@cul.co.uk

I will put all the sample sites, any new information, feedback and anything else relevant on the *Mining the Internet* site:
www.cul.co.uk/mining

QUICK JUMPER

Want something now? Do read the rest of the book, but use this section to jump in at the deep end. It's important before you do that you make sure you are clear just what it is you want. If you've got a little time, read the rest of this chapter to help with that before you plunge in.

Companies

- Web sites – see page 109;
- Locations – see page 104;
- Telephone numbers – see page 110;
- Products – see page 127.

People

- Want to get in touch with someone? – see page 96;
- Telephone numbers – see page 103;
- Addresses – see page 103;
- Biographies – see page 103.

Places

- How to get there – see page 106;
- Maps – see page 104;
- Facilities – see page 107;
- What's on – see page 108.

Reference

- Basic facts – see page 83;
- News – see page 83;
- Weather – see page 91.

Search engine skills

- Finding search engines – see page 40;
- Basic searching – see page 41;
- Using fancy search terms – see page 44.

Internet shopping

- Safety – see page 127;
- Finding the right product – see page 127;
- Software – see page 131.

WHAT THE INTERNET IS

First of all, it's big. It's very big. Imagine a large open space (Texas will do nicely), covered all over with bulletin boards. Millions of them, filled with close-typed sheets of information. Some of it extremely useful, some of it garbage. The chances are, a fair proportion of what you want to know is out there. Somewhere. Of course, you've got to find it, but it needn't be too painful.

At the nuts and bolts level, the Internet is a collection of networks, where a network is a set of computers wired together so they can exchange information. On top of this world-spanning framework sits a whole range of facilities. Electronic mail, the World Wide Web, newsgroups and more.

Try It

Think big

A little exercise to bring home the scale of the Internet. Browse to your favourite search engine. (If you don't have one or don't even know what one is yet, don't worry, all will be revealed – try http://www.altavista.com for now.) Enter a very common word and see how many responses you get back (it will usually tell you somewhere near the top of the search results).

I tried *computer*, using the UK version of AltaVista, and got 66,547,950 pages. And this is just scratching the surface, looking for a single word in every search engine. There are many more pages out there, covering practically any subject you can think of.

At the practical level, the Internet is a communication medium. It's a way of getting information to other people. The people who publish that information have all sorts of different motives. They may be big businesses, wanting to polish their corporate image. They might have something to sell. They might want to show off their expertise in an esoteric subject. They might want to discuss a topic of interest. They might just want to say 'here I am!' As a consumer of the Internet, you need to be aware of just what the person on the other end is about – but given that awareness you can use all these types of communication for your benefit.

Figure 1.1 Searching for 'computer' in the AltaVista Company's AltaVista search engine

WHAT THE INTERNET ISN'T

It's often easier to say what something isn't than what it is. Here's a few highlights of what the Internet isn't.

It isn't a library

At least, not a library as we'd normally think of it. It has a lot of similarities, but look at the differences. There is no organization. There is no universal catalogue. There are no librarians. Imagine a library where anyone could write a book, then throw it in through the window to land wherever it happens to fall. Inside, a bunch of idiot robots are going round trying to index what's there, without bothering to organize the books in any way. At the same time, a set of particularly unpleasant mice is gnawing books to pieces. Oh, and as well as those authors, there are lots of businesses and junk catalogue companies throwing things through the window.

On the plus side, you don't have to be quiet – in fact it can be a fun place. You can skip from reference to reference in seconds. There's no censorship, there's interactivity and there's excitement. The fact that it's not a library has disadvantages, but unless you are a professional library-lover it also has a very positive feeling of liberation. And you don't have to go down to town in the rain to get in.

It isn't all-containing

Nope. It's big, but not that big. There are very significant gaps in the information content of the Internet. Even when there is information, it hasn't gone through the same filtering mechanism as a book. Anyone can put anything on to the Internet. They don't have to know what they are talking about; it doesn't have to be true, and it certainly doesn't have to be comprehensive.

On the other hand, the quality of information is improving all the time, and where once it was the exception to be able to find the information you want this way, now it's increasingly the norm. For that matter, we probably tend to ascribe too much truth to anything we see in 'real' print like a book or a newspaper. Trust me, I'm a writer, I know about these things. The Internet is never going to have everything you need – but it has got an increasingly impressive proportion of it.

It isn't free for all

The Internet began in the late sixties and early seventies, in a young United States that was heavily into free ... pretty well everything. It has always carried this alternative lifestyle image. Yet when it comes down to solid cash, the freedom is illusory. Some of us pay telephone charges and connection charges just to see the thing. While the majority of the information you are liable to need can then be reached without further spending, high quality sources often charge – sometimes a lot.

Having said that, the Internet is considerably freer than practically any other medium. It's relatively free from censorship (with all the pros and cons that carries). Much of the software you need to use it is free. And although some professional information sources do charge, many more put up information without cost that they would charge for via any other medium. It may not be free, but it's remarkably cheap.

It isn't just the World Wide Web

The World Wide Web is the glitzy, highly visible portion of the Internet, but it is only one part. The Internet is a way of getting information across – a transport medium, like radio waves. Just as TV, radio and mobile phones all use this same mechanism, so services like the Web sit on top of the Internet. This is worth establishing so we don't forget all those other good things, but not worth getting too excited about.

It isn't just for nerds

Once upon a time, yes, the Internet was a techie heaven. Unless you could build your own PC from scratch (and probably wire it into the phone system without the telephone company's knowledge) you weren't a real citizen of the Internet. Now everyone's out there. Of course, this doesn't mean that the nerds have gone away – and there is still an odour of sour grapes from those who feel that anything commercial is corrupting – but you can spend a lifetime on the World Wide W eb without encountering nerd-dom. Internet newsgroups and other online forums (I know the plural is 'fora', but not in the online world) still provide breeding grounds for the terminally technical, but if you approach them carefully, they will communicate with lesser mortals.

It isn't full of pornography

Bearing in mind the lack of censorship, the Internet has its share of pornography from the sort of thing that appears in tabloid newspapers to hard-core material that is illegal in many countries. If you use the Internet for any length of time, you will occasionally come across it. You might be sent unsolicited mail advertising it. You may be searching on a perfectly proper topic, and find that your results include some doubtful sounding sites. You may even find a site hiding under an innocent name – at the time of writing, one pornographic Web site uses the same name (but spelled differently) as one of the 'white pages' e-mail directories.

Even so, it's worth keeping the pornographic aspect of the Internet in proportion. The vast majority of sites are not pornographic – in fact, the proportion of pornographic pages is much lower than you would find on the shelves of a typical newsstand. Unless you actively seek it out, you will not get a lot of trouble with pornographic material, and it's worth bearing in mind that even if you accidentally browse to a dubious site, it can't do you any harm – your PC can't be contaminated just by browsing.

The availability of pornography is often of concern to those with children. It is very difficult to totally prevent access (especially as most children are better with computers than their parents). There are, however, products that will help with this by looking out for the typical language of a pornographic site or known addresses, which you can invest in if you like. Alternatively, you can use a product that simply keeps track of which sites have been visited (see page 25 for a do-it-yourself method). If your children are aware that you have this ability, the thought of you looking over their shoulder may well be enough to discourage them.

It isn't boring

The Internet is sometimes described as boring or sad, in the same way that some people will describe practically anything requiring more than four brain cells boring. I find this difficult to understand. As long as you can reach the right places (and that, I admit takes a bit of practice), you will find something that fascinates you, whatever your interests are. That being the case, you have to be terminally uninterested in life to find the Internet boring. I'd dig out that Samuel Johnson quote about being tired of London as a parallel, but you've all heard it before (no? you can find it on the Internet. See page 85).

What is quite possible is that Internet enthusiasts, or those with something to sell, over-hyped it in the early days. When I first used the World Wide Web, for instance, everyone got a thrill out of connecting to a botanical site in Australia, because, wow! we're actually connected to a computer halfway across the world. It was quite exciting the first time – but the only thing that will maintain the excitement is good content, and that was sadly lacking. Now it's a different story. Similarly, a lot of people got excited about developments in the Web as the next step on from television. After all, it was interactive! What they didn't seem to realize is that it was also painfully slow, low resolution and amateurish. When you want to slump in front of the TV, you are not looking for a Web experience. But that doesn't make the Internet boring – just the expectations misguided.

WHAT DO YOU WANT?

So we've got the background on the Internet – time to plunge in? Almost. It's worth spending a few moments clarifying just what it is you intend to look for. Is it a straightforward fact or piece of information – the sort of thing that you would look up in an encyclopedia? If so, see Chapter 7 on quick reference. If it involves a little more, do give yourself a chance to think. Exactly what do you want? Spending half a minute jotting down some detail may save you a lot of time online, as you can come up with more appropriate keywords.

zoom in

Keywords

'Keywords' is a magic term as far as searching the Internet goes. The idea is to distil down just what it is you are looking for into a small number of words. Hopefully, these words will appear in the item you want to find, or a summary of it. The trouble is, the English language is a rich one, and you can use many different words to mean roughly the same thing. When you are jotting down keywords, make sure that you consider different ways of saying something.

Let's say we wanted to find out more about the Austin Seven, a small British car from the 1920s with a cult following in the United States and UK. The obvious keywords are Austin, Seven and car. But after a little thought I might add 7, automobile, vintage, veteran, chummy and so on.

A couple of things are happening here. First, I am looking for alternative ways of saying the same thing – 7 as well as Seven, automobile as well as car. Then I am looking for keywords to home in on my requirement in a different way. Vintage and veteran are terms used for old cars. If you are into old cars you might point out that these are very specific terms which wouldn't apply to all old cars – true, but they will reach the right sort of site, which may link on to an Austin Seven site. The best trick of all is to use some form of special jargon, which is unlikely to be linked with any other possible meaning of the keywords (after all, I don't want vintage wine). Because I know that 'chummy' is a popular term for one type of Austin Seven, it might prove a valuable keyword.

TRY AS YOU GO

The Internet is a hands-on medium. As we travel through the different approaches, don't feel restrained from getting your hands dirty. Try out some of the exercises. If there's something you want to look up for real, use it to test out some of the approaches. Like any skill, becoming a smart Internet navigator requires plenty of practice.

RECAP

The Internet is a brilliant source of information, quick to access, cheap and available where and when you want it. But it can also be confusing – this book is about the skills you need to mine the Internet for information. Remember, though that the Internet isn't a library (it has very little structure), it's not all free, it isn't just the World Wide Web, it's not just for nerds, it's not all pornography and it doesn't have to be boring – if you use it right.

For anything more than a simple piece of information, you will save a lot of online time if you spend a few moments thinking through your requirements and devising sensible keywords first – but don't be scared of trying things out, your skills will improve with practice.

2 SKILLS
Walking the Web

- ■ A quick introduction to the World Wide Web;
- ■ What the Web is good for;
- ■ What the Web is bad for;
- ■ Keeping information after you disconnect.

WHAT IS THIS WORLD WIDE WEB?

This chapter is mainly for those who are new to the World Wide Web. If you know your Internet Explorers from your Netscape Navigators and are comfortable with caching and subscriptions, you might like to skip on to the next chapter.

I'm starting with a stupid question – but sometimes you have to be able to ask stupid questions, because it's assumed everyone knows the answer. What is the World Wide Web? Once upon a time it was a very grandiose title for a system that allowed a small number of researchers in a small number of places to share information – now, though it has fulfilled the promise of that immodest name. Devised by Tim Berners-Lee at the CERN particle physics research centre in Geneva, the Web amalgamated a number of existing concepts.

The Web starts with the Internet. As we've already seen, the two aren't the same thing, whatever impression you get from the mass media. The Internet is a mechanism for enabling millions of linked computers to interchange information. The Web is a specific use of the Internet, a mechanism for retrieving information that uses the Internet as a connection. Again, this is nothing new – one of the very first developments on the Internet was FTP, File Transfer Protocol. The Web uses a different protocol, HTTP (HyperText Transfer Protocol), hence the HTTP:// bit at the start of the address you use to find a Web site, with a rather different approach, but the basic idea is similar.

Protocols

You might think quite reasonably that protocols are the business of diplomats, but the term was borrowed by the computer world before the Internet existed. As soon as computers began to be connected together they needed a way of interchanging information. Because each make of computer worked a different way, there had to be a standard 'language' of intercommunication. Protocols define the way these interchanges go ahead. The earliest protocols were for direct computer-to-computer communication, soon followed by FTP (see page 34) in 1972.

Probably the cleverest thing about the way the Web was devised was the use of hypertext. (No, not the graphics, which was probably why it then took off in a big way. That came later.) Again, hypertext is nothing new. Books are essentially great big straight lines of text, folded up to fit on pages. You may jump around in a reference book using an index, but usually you start at the beginning and work through to the end. Hypertext (a term coined by Ted Nelson, a 1960s computer visionary) is different. Various bits of the text can point to various other bits. Say you were talking about steam engines and wanted to refer the reader to a biographical article on James Stephenson elsewhere in the book. In a conventional text you would say 'see page 68'. Hypertext gives you a direct link – you just click from where you are and jump to the new location. Instead of the straight line of a book, a hypertext document is like a mess of pieces of string – a network or a web.

There were hypertext programs on our computers before the World Wide Web. The package Hypercard on the Apple Macintosh popularized the approach, while the Windows help system on the PC has always been an easy-to-use but painful-to-write hypertext system. By picking up on the idea of hypertext links, the Web became much more than a way of retrieving obscure documents; it is a three-dimensional publishing environment, where documents aren't totally separate items, but can be tied together into a world-spanning whole. Very quickly, the bells and whistles started to be added to make the Web graphical, and the modern phenomenon was born.

Browsers

The software used to view the Web is referred to as a browser. Unlike most computer software, browsers are (on the whole) free. You will usually be provided with one when you connect up to the Internet. If your version is out-of-date, you can update (unless you use a service where a modified browser is built into a special program) from the Internet or from cover disks of computer magazines, which generally carry the latest versions.

The two big names in the browser field are Netscape and Microsoft. Netscape's Navigator (still called this, but it is now part of the larger Communicator) was the first really commercial browser, which originally dominated the market. Microsoft's Internet Explorer rapidly caught up with extra features (and by being free). Both are distant cousins of the earliest graphical browser, Mosaic.

Both browsers are very good and continue to develop. For this book Navigator version 6 and Internet Explorer version 5.5 were used. Some of the features described here may not be available in older versions. To check out the latest possibilities, visit the Web sites:

Netscape – www.netscape.com/download
Microsoft – www.microsoft.com/ie

WEB SITES

Where, then, do Web sites come into this picture? Although instant, easy linkages can give the impression that the Web is one big place, it exists on a huge collection of computers – many, but not all of the computers that make up the Internet. When you look at the Web, you are looking at a page – in effect a document – and each page is physically located in a Web site. A site is a collection of pages, usually on the same computer, which are all owned by the same person or organization. You could think of a Web site as a book, made up of the combined pages, or a filing cabinet full of documents. Because of the way the Web works, when you click on a link it could take you to a different page in the same site or to a page halfway across the world – it makes no difference – but within a site you will generally see more consistency of approach. Sites are often subject-oriented, providing information on different aspects of a particular topic, but that's a matter of the owner's taste. Remember, there aren't any rules about the content of the Web – there's nothing to stop each page being totally unrelated.

In principle, a whole site could consist of a single page. This isn't quite as unwieldy as it sounds, as links can work within a page as well as from page to page. In practice, though, it's popular to keep pages quite short, as the longer the page is, the longer it takes to download – and no one wants to sit around waiting.

WHAT'S THE WEB GOOD FOR?

The Web is the ultimate skimmer's tool. The most popular terms for getting information from the Web are browsing and surfing, but neither really captures the reality. Browsing sounds dull and slow. Surfing was no doubt used to typify the laid-back Californian feel that was common in the early days, but it's not all that appropriate. After all, surfing doesn't get you anywhere but back where you started from. What the Web enables you to do is skim the surface of information, skipping from location to location like a stone spun over the surface of water. In half a minute you can move around the world, and have changed topics half a dozen times.

This jumping from place to place, from subject to subject, may not be very practical, but it can be fascinating. It's a great way to spend an hour if you want to see something different. The Web is also good for buying things and for getting hold of information. Web shopping was something of a mystery to begin with. Companies nervously put up a small percentage of their merchandise, found few buyers and decided it wasn't going to work. They totally missed out on the fact that the advantage of an electronic shop over the real thing is that the floor area is vast. An electronic shop can and should carry many more products than a physical one, not less. It needs to make up for its poor browsing facilities – nothing like the real thing – by offering superb searching and linking, something a real shop can't provide. That's why book and CD stores were amongst the first to really take off. The big product range, with limited need to actually touch the merchandise before you buy it, made them ideal.

WHAT'S THE WEB BAD AT?

Such is the excitement about the Internet, and the Web in particular, that it is being seen as many things that it really isn't, and isn't suitable for. Media companies, eager to stick with the familiar, have tried treating the Web as a set of TV channels. Others have looked at the Web as if they were publishing a magazine. But neither of these approaches works very well. Unlike other media, the hold the site has on its readers is very tenuous. It may only be seconds before they skip off elsewhere. Yes, they may stay and read something, or listen to some sound, but the next page they turn to may well be in a totally different publication. This means rather strangely that, though the Web is as much of a revolution in publishing as was the printing press, it isn't ideal for traditional book or magazine publishing.

The On-Line Books Page

EST. 1993 - UPDATED JANUARY 12, 2001 - FREE

BOOKS ON-LINE

Search our 13,000+ Listings -- New Listings -- Authors -- Titles -- Subjects -- Serials

NEWS

Celebration of Women Writers now at Penn -- Celebrating 10,000 Free On-Line Books -- Latest Book Listings

FEATURES

A Celebration of Women Writers -- Banned Books On-Line -- Prize Winners On-Line (in preparation)

ARCHIVES

General -- Foreign Language -- Specialty

THE INSIDE STORY

About Us -- FAQ -- Get Involved! -- Books In Progress/Requested -- More Book Links

Figure 2.1 Searchable database of online books (On-Line Books Page)

This doesn't mean you won't find books on the Web. Increasingly you will find full texts of classic works available. Publishers of e-books (see page 95) provide new titles online, usually to be downloaded at a price. But it isn't a place to sit down and read a novel, or a magazine. A snippet, yes. A review or some words of wisdom. But not a full volume. Having the full text of books available is great, but people are much more likely to download them to their PCs for later dissection than to try to read them online.

Sample Sites

Classic books online

If you are interested in getting hold of the text of a book – perhaps you've always wanted to know how many times 'and' appears in the works of Jane Austen – there are a number of sites specializing in this. Most, if not all of the books will be quite old, as they need to be out of copyright before they can legally be bandied about in this way. Much of what you will find is heavy duty literature, but there is some light stuff too – for example, Project Bartleby includes the complete works of Agatha Christie.

- Bibliobytes – www.bb.com
- Bibliomania – www.bibliomania.com
- Internet Classics Archive – classics.mit.edu
- Online Medieval & Classics Library – sunsite.berkeley.edu/OMACL
- The Online Books Page (13,000+ titles) – digital.library.upenn.edu/books
- Project Bartleby Archive – www.columbia.edu/acis/bartleby
- Project Gutenberg – www.gutenberg.net

MOVING AROUND A SITE

Do you like standards? Do you like the Apple Mac or Windows interface on your PC because you'll always find certain things in the same place? You're going to hate the Web. About the only standard is that there aren't real standards. (This patently isn't true, but all the standards are under the hood, about how computers talk to each other or the language used to lay out the page.) Imagine what it would be like if every car you needed to drive had all the controls in different places, and half of them were completely hidden. That's the experience that you get when dealing with a Web site.

Unlike a Windows or Mac programmer who has quite strict rules about what should do what, the Web site designer is unfettered by such minor considerations as usability by normal human beings. Luckily though, while there aren't standards or even conventions, there are style trends. Sometimes Web sites seem to occupy the world of fashion rather than information technology. Once a trend is set, everyone follows slavishly. This means that on the whole you can get around relatively painlessly.

Although (good) Web sites aren't organized like books, you will usually find some form of contents structure. It might be a site map – a pictorial representation of what's on the site. It might be a set of 'chapter' headings, usually down the side or along the top of the screen. These provide high-level navigation, while individual links within the pages get you around at a detailed level. Many sites also have a search facility, where you can look for the occurrence of anything on the site – in effect, an index covering every word.

Try It

A painless beginning

If you haven't already, try finding the *Mining the Internet* site. You'll find any new information since the book was published, feedback from readers, and links to many of the sites referenced in this book – saves you all that irritating typing! Just click in your browser's address box and type:

www.cul.co.uk/mining

Then press the Enter key. On older browsers you may have to stick http:// in front of the address. If you're new to the Web, have a look at the basic navigation primer. Otherwise, just take a look around the site for useful pointers.

The important thing about navigation in a site (in fact about navigating the Web as a whole) is being prepared to explore. Don't spend ages pondering which is the right link to click – grab one and have a look. If you don't like what you see, you've a handy 'Back' button on your browser to go back to where you just came from and try again.

GETTING AROUND THE WEB (AND THE WORLD)

Looking at a single site, however impressive, doesn't give you a taste of the real Web. Sometimes one site will be enough – you might just need to look up something and get straight out, but the big benefit of all the clever hypertext linking is the way you can follow a link to a totally different place and get associated but different information.

Doing so is stunningly easy – in fact, it's no different from moving around within a site. Just click on a link – it can take you anywhere from a different point on the same page to the other side of the world. Links to other sites take a little longer usually (though not much – delays are usually down to slow lines or slow servers, not the need to link elsewhere). Because of this ease of connection, most Web sites have links to other sites on associated topics – frequently these are helpfully labelled 'links'.

Often, given a starting point, this leaping from site to site is enough to fill in everything you need – but you do need that starting point. This is where search engines (of which much more in Chapter 4) come in. There's no such thing as a definitive index of the Web, but the search engines are the next best thing – and considering how much information they deal with, they're stunningly quick. With the right techniques, search engines and other Web tools, you will soon be painlessly circling the globe to find the information you want.

PROTECTED SITES – FREE AND PAYING

Sooner or later as you wander around the Web you will come across a site that doesn't just let you in. Usually they will ask for a logon and password – a check to see who you are. This shouldn't be too surprising.

The Internet isn't a public utility, even if many sites are provided by public bodies. A great many sites belong to businesses, who aren't going to spend good money without a return. That doesn't mean that all commercial sites are protected in this way. For many, it's enough to increase your awareness of their products and presence. The same sort of argument as advertising on commercial television. But others want more.

Don't panic, though, if a site you want to get into requires you to 'register' or 'subscribe'. This doesn't necessarily mean that you are going to be asked to cough up cash. And remember that there is no way that a Web site can see into your Internet service provider's account and extract your credit card details. Even if a site does end up asking for money, you can simply ignore it. You won't get in – but you won't lose any cash.

zoom in

Relationship marketing

Once upon a time, companies knew nothing about their customers. An individual would come into the shop, buy a few things, go through the door and that was that. They might come in every week, they might never return – but the shopkeeper wouldn't know the difference. Now this isn't such a good thing. Businesses began to realize that customers have a 'lifetime value'. You might think Miss Wiggins isn't worth the time of day, because she only ever spends £5 at a time. But what if she spends it every week. For 20 years. All of a sudden, she's worth not £5, but £5,000 – quite a different prospect.

At the same time, businesses knew they were wasting vast amounts of money on mailshots and advertising which was of no interest to most of the people who received it. Enter relationship marketing. If you can identify individual customers and know something about them, everyone wins. The customer gets better service because you can tailor your service (and advertising). The businesses win because they keep the customers. Relationship marketing is the whole reason for Marks and Spencer bringing out a shopping card (and why for so long they didn't accept credit cards). It's the reason behind customer loyalty cards at supermarkets and frequent flyer schemes. Yes, it gets companies a bit more revenue because there's an incentive to use them, but more importantly they find out about the customer.

In theory, the Web is the ideal vehicle for relationship marketing because a lot of the requirements can be automated. Whether appearing as registration or as clever services like e-mails that tell you when your favourite author has a new book out, relationship marketing is a major Web phenomenon.

It's reasonable to ask, if a site isn't asking for money, what's the point of this registration business? It's all about relationship marketing. See the Zoom in box if you want to know more – in essence they want to know more about you so that they can try build up a relationship (however tenuous) with you to increase the chances of getting money out of you in the future.

Some sites are different, though. They want money up front. This can be on a subscription basis or a charge each time you use the service. Don't entirely dismiss charging services because you think that the Web ought to be free. Remember, the people on the other end need to earn a living. And sometimes the information you are getting access to is worth paying for. Anyone with an interest in US business, for instance, might think it worth paying to have access to the *Wall Street Journal*, interactive edition. You pays your money (or don't) and takes your choice.

WHERE IS EVERYONE?

As should be obvious by now, the Web is a big, tangled mess. In Chapter 4 we will look at search engines in detail. But it's worth getting some groundwork in early on simple navigation. As we have seen, you can go to a Web site by typing in its address. That's fine if you saw it on the TV or read it in a magazine, but what if you want to access a site without having the address?

The good news is that, unlike a postal address, you've a fair chance of guessing it. That's because Web addresses have a standardized format. In fact, the real address is a set of impenetrable numbers, but this is covered up by a human-friendly address with an unfriendly name: Uniform Resource Locators (URLs). They all start HTTP:// – HTTP for Hyper-Text Transfer Protocol, the colon (:) to show that the 'protocol' part of the address has finished (see Zoom in on Protocols on page 13) and the two slashes to say that this is the start of a network address – a location on a computer network. Modern Web browsers will generally put that bit in for you, so you needn't type it. For this reason it is omitted from the addresses of sample sites in this book, but it's still there really.

Next there's usually www (no prizes for guessing this stands for World Wide Web). Technically there was no need to have this bit, but most people put it in their address now because … most people put it in their address (sigh). Then there will be something to identify the company or organization. And finally an ending which determines what sort of organization we are dealing with, and what country it is located in (possibly – see the Zoom in on Endings below for more information).

So, let's say you wanted to guess the address of a company called The Big Company. It's a no-brainer to type www. (It isn't always necessary, but often is, and it is almost always accepted.) Then an appropriate name for the company. Finally end up with .com for a US company or .co.xx for other countries (eg .co.uk). Bear in mind that .com is popular in non-US countries too, so always try that. As you'll see in the Endings Zoom in, there are other possible endings – you can go on to these if you don't get anywhere. Guessing the form of the company's name may take a few tries. For instance, it could be:

- www.thebigcompany.com
- www.bigcompany.com
- www.tbc.com
- www.bc.com
- www.bigco.com

or any of these ending .co.uk … or most of these with hyphens (-), underscores (_) or dots (.) between the names. This might seem an awful lot of possible combinations, but very often when you try something obvious like www.sony.com or www.microsoft.com it works. Part of the reason it's not always obvious is that the name might be too long. I use www.cul.co.uk for my company because no one could be bothered to type www.creativityunleashedlimited.co.uk and anyway a three-letter address is a bit like a personalized number plate. Some companies were unlucky – someone else with a legitimate claim got the obvious address first. If, however, you are trying to hit a car manufacturer and you see the page of a careers service start to appear, don't immediately try typing something else – scan that page. It's quite often the case that when a Web site sounds like it could be for a well-known name, the owner gives you a courtesy link to where you really want to go: take a look first.

Endings

The Internet has a specific set of endings for addresses, which are supposed to determine just what type of organization you are dealing with. These include:

- .ac/.edu – academic (universities, colleges, etc)
- .co/.com – company
- .gov – government
- .mil – military
- .net – network company/service provider
- .org – other non-business organization
- .sch – school

Just as UK postage stamps are the only ones in the world without the country name, because they originated here, these endings are technically the US ones. Other countries are supposed to have a modified version that shows which country they are (if there are two options, use the shorter one when followed by a country identifier). For instance .com becomes .co.uk in the UK. Confusingly, however, there is nothing to stop a UK company from having a US ending – it just shows who the site pays for the address. Many non-US companies do choose to use their country's ending, though. Common ones are:

- .au – Australia
- .de – Germany
- .fr – France
- .uk – United Kingdom

To confuse matters even more, many smaller countries don't bother with the .co (or whatever), and a whole extra set of endings are under constant debate. .ltd and .plc can be used for an address that matches the company's registered name, but are still uncommon as they are unlikely to be guessed. Other recent extensions are .biz, .name, .info and .pro. Others could be anything from .news to .sex – keep your eyes open.

THE LANGUAGE BARRIER

You might think that a worldwide system would make it difficult to understand much of the Web. However, a combination of the US origins of the Internet and the long-standing tradition of using English for international academic conferences and as the language of international business means that a high percentage of sites are in English. Even when a site is in another language, the site's owners will often bow to the market and have an English version.

This means that English speakers are very fortunate when it comes to getting the most from the Web. Sometimes, though, you will find a site that is only available in a foreign language. Luckily, there are freely available mechanisms for automatic translation – for example, the search engine AltaVista will translate a Web page from the most popular languages while keeping all the format of the page. If you don't like the free products, there are also software products to run on your PC which perform automatic translation, some linking directly into your Web browser, so the page is presented as normal, but with English words. A good example is Power Translator Professional from Lernout & Hauspie – see www.lhsl.com/powertranslator for more details.

You can also use these translators to convert your letters and e-mails to another language, but bear in mind whatever you are using them for that automatic translation can only go so far. The result may be understandable, but it is unlikely to read naturally, and may be hilarious. To get some idea of what may be happening, try translating a document back into English and see how it reads.

Stille Nacht

Sometimes, when dealing with a foreign language it is worth remembering that the majority of the Web is aimed at English-speaking audiences, so even a search involving a foreign language topic may be best expressed in English. I was asked to help someone who was looking for the German words to the carol 'Silent night'. The enquirer knew that the original German carol was called *'Stille Nacht'*, and had entered this into a search engine, without finding appropriate results. We tried again with the search term *"silent night" german* – forcing the engine to look for the phrase 'silent night' with the inverted commas. The first four responses all gave the German words of the carol – one even had the sheet music.

WHERE'D IT GO?

Most of us have a bit of a shock early on in our experience of using the Web. You do a little browsing around, then come offline to let your phone bill have a rest. You flip back over a couple of the pages you've looked at, then close the browser. A little later, you remember something you'd like to check out, and reopen browser. Only there's nothing left in your Back button – you can't go back to what you looked at earlier. Luckily, your browser has a History button, so you choose one of the pages, and it promptly asks to go back online. It can be a real frustration – why isn't the information still there?

Try It

Cache secrets

You wouldn't normally look at your cache directly, but just out of curiosity, take a look at what's in there. There are specifics below on finding the cache for the two big name browsers – whatever browser you use ought to specify somewhere where it holds its cache. Note just how many files there are – often extending back a lot further than your browser's history. Bear this in mind, if for any reason you might visit a site you don't want others to know about (for instance, a job search page) – anything you've looked at may be lurking on your machine for months. These examples are Windows versions, but other operating systems should have equivalents.

Internet Explorer – choose Internet Options from the Tools Menu. Click the Settings button in the Temporary Internet Files section. In the middle of the next screen you should see a line identifying the current folder. You'll find when you look in it with Windows Explorer that there may be several sub-folders, all bulging with Web documents and pictures.

Netscape Navigator – in the latest version of Navigator the cache location is not displayed in the program, but by default it can be found (Windows version) in the Mozilla folder within the Application Data folder that sits in the Windows folder. In older versions of Navigator the cache location was shown in the advanced section of the preferences, viewed from the Edit menu.

In fact it probably is, which is where the rather grandly named cache comes in. My dictionary defines a cache as a hiding place for treasure, a hoard, a secret store of something or other. This isn't a bad term to use. A cache is just a set of directories (folders to youthful readers) where the browser keeps a copy of things it looks at so it doesn't have to go back to the Web every time it wants them. It isn't really designed to be looked at by human beings, but you will find it in your browser settings so that you can control how much space you allocate to cache. I like to have plenty of space so I can get back a page over quite a period. Luckily, software vendors have finally caught on to the fact that mere mortals like us have to pay for our phone bills, and so are making the cache a lot more practical to use.

KEEPING WEB DATA AFTER YOU DISCONNECT

Although the cache has always stayed around, early Web browsers tended to ignore it. A small but thriving market developed for products that allowed you to search your cache, or keep a practical memory of what you had looked at. Now it can be much easier.

Why is the cache so reticent? Why doesn't it pop up when you try to revisit a site from your history? In fact it could if you wanted it to. Delve into your browser settings and you will find options to force the cache into operation. For instance, in Internet Explorer, look at Internet Options. You will see a button for Settings of Temporary Internet Pages (they think the term 'cache' is too technical and/or short). It gives the option of checking for newer versions of stored pages every time you visit the page, every time you start Internet Explorer (usually the case) or never. Set it to 'never' and you'll go straight to the cache when you choose a page in history. But this ignores the fluidity of the Web. A lot might have changed – you don't always want this to happen.

To keep the balance right, some browsers are now a lot smarter. If you pull up a page from your history and the browser tries to connect to the Internet, cancel the connection. If you have a modern product you will find that it switches into 'offline' mode and looks in the cache instead (there's also a menu item to force this to happen). You will now move around in the cache until you choose a page that isn't on your PC – then you will be given the option of connecting up to the Internet again. Smart stuff. This feature was introduced in Internet Explorer version 4, and Navigator version 4.5.

If you have a reasonable sized cache, your data will stay around for weeks – which makes it very practical to scan sites of interest, then come offline and digest the content at your leisure. Make sure a page is fully loaded (all the pictures showing, if you want pictures) before you move on – you will only see offline what you see online, and may even see less. As an alternative to this 'manual' approach, some Web browsers like Internet Explorer allow you to 'subscribe' to a site. This doesn't involve signing up with the site. Instead, your browser will, on a scheduled basis or manually, connect up to the site and download the latest version of the page. An additional option here is to also download pages that the selected page is linked to, making it easier to scan a chunk of a site offline, rather than just the first page.

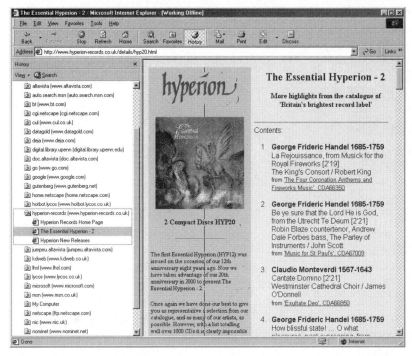

Figure 2.2 Internet Explorer's history in action

Try It

History

If you've already done some browsing, check out your history. (If you haven't, do some exploration from the *Mining the Internet* site (see page 18 for details), then look at the history.) The instructions below work with the two best-known browsers – if you use another, check the menus for 'History' or try the online help.

Internet Explorer – Start Internet Explorer. If it tries to connect to the Internet, cancel the connection. Look in the File menu and make sure that the Work Offline entry (near the bottom) is checked (has a tick against it) – choose the option from the menu if it hasn't. Now click the History button. A bar appears on the left of the screen detailing the pages you have visited recently. These pages can be searched and arranged by date or name using the View button. Look at a few. Note what happens if you click on a link in a page – if you used it when you visited, it will work. If not, you will be given the option of going online and getting the page. Explore your history.

Netscape Navigator – Start Navigator. If it tries to connect to the Internet, cancel the connection. Look in the Offline item of the Files menu. If it says 'Work Offline', choose it, so it now reads 'Work Online'. Choose History from the Tools item in the Tasks menu (previously in the Communicator menu). You will see a list of pages you have visited. Try going back to some of the pages you have already seen. You will find some are available, others will tell you that you are unable to connect to the network.

SECURITY

There's nothing the press likes better than a breach of security. Whether it's a matter of viruses taking over your computer or nasty people stealing your credit card number, computer security is a headline issue. As a Web user you have two possible security worries. The first concerns cookies. These are little files placed on your computer to hold information, so that next time you go back to the site it can remember what you did last time. This can be very helpful. It can save you from typing lots of information in, and provide handy tailored pages. However, it can also be used to target marketing in your direction, and it worries some people because they don't like the thought of an external source being able to write files (however innocuous) on to your PC. Most browsers will give you the choice whether or not to accept cookies. I find the advantages of personalization (some sites simply won't work without a cookie) out-weigh any potential dangers – but it's a personal choice.

The second Web security issue is over payment. At some point in your Web wanderings, whether looking to buy something or not, you are liable to come across a screen inviting you to type in your credit card details. First, a reassurance. Although you will probably have given your credit card details to your Internet service provider (ISP), they are not visible to a Web site – they can't get your credit card details without your help. So let's assume you actually want to buy – is it safe to type in those numbers? Inevitably the answer is yes and no.

If the site has no form of security, the answer is a straight no. The Internet is too open to be happy about sending credit card details around willy-nilly. Bearing in mind that e-mail has very little security, it might be worth extending that restriction to e-mails – it's safest not to e-mail someone your details. How do you know if a site is secure? The site will usually say – if it doesn't you might like to assume it's not. Also, at the point when you are about to type in details, your Web browser will have to go into secure mode. Look for a lock or key in the bar at the bottom of the browser. This indicates that the site is using SSL (Secure Socket Layer), which encrypts your information into an unreadable mess before sending it across the Internet.

The mere fact of using SSL doesn't provide total, cast-iron security. For example, do you know the company is who they say they are? Are they respectable? However, it's fair to say that once you know there is SSL, you can have as much if not more confidence in the safety of using your credit card details this way as you would of using them over the phone. If you are still concerned, any good retailer will offer alternatives – for example, ordering on the site, but sending payment via fax or through the post. Others have an approach where you set up an account with them – once you've done that, you don't need to use your credit card number, just your account number, which is meaningless elsewhere.

BOOKMARKS, FAVOURITE PLACES AND SHORTCUTS

Most of this book is about finding the sites and information you need. Some of your searches will be one-offs. But often you will find a site that you want to come back to. Luckily, modern browsers are well equipped to keep track of where you have been to make it easy to get back. I would strongly recommend you to use one of these techniques to keep track of any site that seems of even the faintest future interest. There's nothing more frustrating than knowing you visited a really handy site a month ago and being unable to get back.

So how do you go about keeping track? You could write all your favourite sites down in a book, but that would get tedious. Slightly more realistic would be copying the addresses from your browser (you should be able to copy it from most browsers) and pasting it into a word processor. Many modern word processors provide 'live' Web links, so you could build up a document with all your favourite links in, then just click on a link in the word processor and get transported there.

In fact, an even more sophisticated variant on this approach would be to save the document in HTML format (an option with most modern word processors). You could then make that document your home page – the page your browser opens when it starts, and returns to when you press the Home button. If you aren't sure how to do this, see the Home page Zoom in. Now you will have your favourite location list appear on screen each time you start the browser.

For most of us, it's enough to make use of bookmarks (or favourites) and shortcuts. Bookmarks (Netscape-speak) and favourites (Microsoft-speak) provide simple pointers to Web sites. They are arranged within the browser in a structure of folders, just like files on your PC. You can use this structure to store your bookmarks in a more effective manner, making it easier to get to just the right site. Usually, browsers come with a bookmark/favourite structure already set up. Feel free to modify this to the structure which most appeals to you – it isn't set in concrete. Both main browsers let you add the page you are currently looking at to your bookmarks – Netscape goes one further in allowing you to type in an address as well.

Home page

When you start your Web browser or click on the friendly Home button, it will usually take you either to a site belonging to the browser's company, or to your Internet service provider. This might suit you fine, but there are plenty of other places you might like to start. Perhaps a favourite search engine, or a document on your PC with your favourite sites on it. Changing your home page is quite possible, and worth the few seconds of effort it takes. If these instructions don't work for you, check the help for your particular browser.

Internet Explorer: make sure you are looking at the page you want to become your home page. If it's on the Web, navigate to it normally. If it's on your PC, select Open from the File menu, then click on the Browse button to find the file. Then choose Internet Options from the Tools menu. If the box that appears doesn't show the 'General' tab, click on that first. At the top is a section headed 'home page' with a button that says Use Current. Click the button. From then on, the page you chose will be your home page.

Netscape Navigator: if the page is on the Web navigate to it in the usual way. In either case, then choose Preferences from the Edit menu. Make sure the 'Navigator' heading is highlighted in the categories box on the left. The top panel says what Navigator starts with – choose Home page. The middle section specifies which page. To use the Web page you are viewing, click the Use Current Page option. To find a file on your PC, click the Choose File button.

Note that most browsers will let you have a blank screen as home page, but this is a waste of a useful facility.

For Windows users, shortcuts are an alternative way of keeping important Web sites. From either of the main browsers you can drag the little icon to the left of the address on to your desktop. It will now appear as a shortcut, just like the shortcuts to programs and files. However, when you open this shortcut, you don't see a file, your Web browser runs and goes to that particular page. If you use some sites all the time, this is an easy way of getting to them in double quick time.

All this is fine, but what if you realize after your visit that you should have marked a site, but you forgot? As we've already seen, you can use your history feature to revisit a page, and bookmark it then.

RECAP

The Web is one of the services on the Internet, along with e-mail, newsgroups and more. It's great for skimming, for finding specific information and for buying items that don't take much browsing. It isn't a substitute for books, magazines or TV. Moving from site to site just takes a click – though you will find some sites where payment is required before you can go far.

Although the Web is a tangled mess, you can often guess a company's Web address, and facilities like search engines and subject indexes can point you in the right direction. Once you've found something you are interested in, it may disappear when you shut down your browser, but the cache and history, combined with judicious use of bookmarks (favourites) should bring back those important pages with a minimum of effort. Security is potentially an issue, but making sure that you don't give any important details to anything other than a secure, trusted site will make the Web as safe a place as any.

3 SKILLS
The Internet beyond the Web

- ■ The wider world of the Internet;
- ■ The importance of people.

THERE'S MORE

The World Wide Web is certainly the flashiest part of the Internet with the most exposure in the media, but it's not the only part of the online world that can help in your search for information. This chapter will introduce some of the other inhabitants of the Internet.

USING PEOPLE

If you use a real library, you may well consult a librarian. If you are look-ing for help – advice perhaps – you usually turn to an expert. The same can be true on the Internet. It's not just a publishing vehicle, it's a way of communicating. In fact, despite all the hype about the Web, the Internet's quiet provision of a channel for e-mail to flow around the world is probably its greatest benefit.

You'll find a full chapter (Chapter 6) a little later on the practicalities of getting help from other people using the Internet. For the moment we'll just get a broad understanding of what's available. E-mail, we've already seen, is an amazing resource. Another possibility is newsgroups.

Newsgroups are generally treated rather warily by Internet newcomers (if they've heard of them at all). There are two reasons they have bad names – because there's a lot of dubious material there, and because contributors tend to be very cliquey. The fact remains that these electronic discussions are a handy source of expertise. Rather than look for a particular piece of information, you can post a request that will be seen by people interested in the subject – and quite possibly get a very helpful answer. See Chapter 6 for more on e-mail, newsgroups, chat and other ways of reaching real people via the Internet.

FTP

File Transfer Protocol (FTP) is one of the oldest facilities on the Internet, even predating e-mail. In effect, FTP is a long-distance version of a file management program – something like Windows Explorer or the Mac Finder that can handle files on other people's computers.

Having said it's like Explorer or Finder, FTP itself is only a very basic definition of how files are to be handled. Just what your FTP will look like depends on who wrote the program you are running to use it. Windows, for instance, comes with a very basic 'command line' FTP which is even less friendly than DOS, while other FTP packages have all the tree and icon user-friendliness of a modern file handling tool.

FTP is a sort of Cinderella that never quite got to the ball. Lack of interest has kept it shabby. Knowing a lot about it has become less important, because almost all the files you want to get hold of are likely to be available directly from a Web site anyway. The mechanism for transferring them to your PC may still be FTP, but you don't care, you just click on the file on the Web page and everything happens. Because FTP is a two-way process (you can use it to put files somewhere else, as well as get hold of them), it is still sometimes used explicitly, but for our purposes it is almost redundant. Some ISPs' software (AOL and CompuServe, for example) have FTP facilities built in, but hidden well away. Otherwise, if you find you need to use it, you may be best downloading a free or shareware graphical FTP package to reduce the strain.

One last consideration – like some Web sites, many FTP sites are secured. Sometimes this means you can only download files (or only upload them). Sometimes it means you need a logon and password to get in.

TELNET

Another of the golden oldies, Telnet represents more of the original vision of the purpose of the Internet than any other facility. Bear in mind that the Internet (and its first component, ARPANET), predates personal computers. The original picture was of a network of large mainframe computers. Such computers are generally used by connecting many terminals (basically a screen and keyboard without any real computing power, often called a 'dumb terminal' because of this) to the computer. The Internet was designed to allow terminals to be switched between different computers sited anywhere geographically, to allow such computers to interact, and to allow files to be transferred (FTP). E-mail, which rapidly became the dominant traffic, was never thought of, while the Web wasn't even a dream.

The program used to connect a terminal to a computer across the Internet is Telnet. It is still available today, and though the Web has reduced the need to use it, it is still occasionally valuable to be able to make direct access to a specific computer in its own specific way. This isn't something you are going to do without guidance – practically every computer has its own little quirks when it comes to connecting up and getting information out – but it is possible, especially if you are engaged in academic research, that you may still need Telnet. The basic Telnet program comes with Windows – like FTP, you may find it helpful to get hold of a product with a more sophisticated interface if you are liable to make significant use of it.

PROPRIETARY SERVICES

Proprietary services cover a multitude of possibilities. Some of the big names for connection to the Internet, like AOL and CompuServe, started as private networks, keeping all the information they provided on their own computers. As these companies moved into selling Internet access, they have maintained their own, separate services, often involving forums and specially formatted information like AOL's weather service.

Increasingly, these features are being moved to the Web, in the form of sites which are only accessible to members of the particular service provider, a specialized form of the protected sites mentioned on page 19, but some remain separate. If you already have an ISP to connect you to the Web, you are unlikely to want one of these services as well, so providing Web addresses is rather pointless. However, most computing magazines with cover disks include software for accessing the big names – use one of these to get some more information on what a proprietary service can offer.

Another type of proprietary services pre-dates the World Wide Web. Such services involve dialling into the service owner's computer, either directly (which can be expensive if the computer is located in another country) or using Telnet. Once connected to the computer you are running an entirely different piece of software, and will have to deal with its individual peculiarities. Most such services involve a considerable subscription and are outside the scope of this book. Almost all services of general value have now been replaced by Web equivalents. For example, the BT Phonebase directory service in the UK has been replaced by BT's online PhoneNet at www.phonenet.uk.bt.com.

RECAP

The Web isn't all there is to the Internet. The most powerful resource out there is people – the people you can reach via e-mail and bulletin boards like the Usenet Newsgroups. There are various other facilities like FTP to transfer files, and Telnet to log on to remote computers, but they are required much less frequently now. You may also find privately owned information on the Internet and via other dial-up services.

4 SKILLS

Search engines and indexes

- Finding what you need;
- Search engines and indexes;
- Simple and sophisticated searching;
- Extra facilities from portal sites.

I'M LOST

Once you have got over the initial thrill of being connected to a Web site halfway across the world, you want something more. It's fine to type in a Web address you found in a magazine and study the exciting dung-beetle site (or whatever). You can even follow links to other dung-beetle sites. But after while, you want something that you don't have an address for, and can't guess just from a name.

Luckily it's a problem that has been recognized almost as long as the Web has been around. If you haven't got a specific address, you are probably best starting off at a portal. This is a fancy term for a way into the Web – pretentious names aren't uncommon, as the term 'search engine' for the most common way of finding information proves. (Search engine is probably a romantic reference to the earliest mechanical computers, which were referred to as 'calculating engines'.) Search engines – which hunt around the Web for items to index, then allow very fast searching of all the information they have retrieved – are very handy tools, though not the only resource available by any means.

KNOCK, KNOCK

A portal is a doorway into the Web, which has the advantage of some sort of structure. Some Internet service providers have their own portal sites, which provide links to very specific hot sites (hot probably being defined as those that are paying them). As well as the ISP's portals, there are independent sites that link out to the Web. Some are specific to a particular subject area – perhaps just for medical matters. Some are structured indexes, which allow you to look at Web content under various categories. Some are search engines that go out on to the Web, find information and organize it, often indexing every word on the site.

While each type of site has its merits, much of this chapter will be concerned with search engines. The concept is great – especially with an in-depth engine like AltaVista, which keeps a note of every word on a site that it looks at. However, search engines do have limitations. They are inevitably out-of-date – it takes days or even weeks to scan the Web. In fact it's worse than that, because none of them will actually scan the whole works – there will always be holes. There is also the reverse problem of being too comprehensive. You might know that when you type in 'computer' you want to know about connecting a joystick to a Dell PC. Unfortunately the search engine doesn't, and will merrily try to list every single page that has the word 'computer' in it – not surprisingly, rather a lot of pages.

zoom in

Don't panic

It is necessary to put up all these warnings and caveats about the limitations of search engines. It makes sense – but don't let it put you off. If you ask for something which occurs half a million times, you won't have to wait while the search engine lists half a million pages – it will tell you how many it has found, but will only show details of the first 10 or 20. As is often the case with hands-dirty use of computers, one of the worst problems with using the Web is fear of getting something wrong. There's no need to be scared – have a go and see what happens. The *try it* boxes below will help with this.

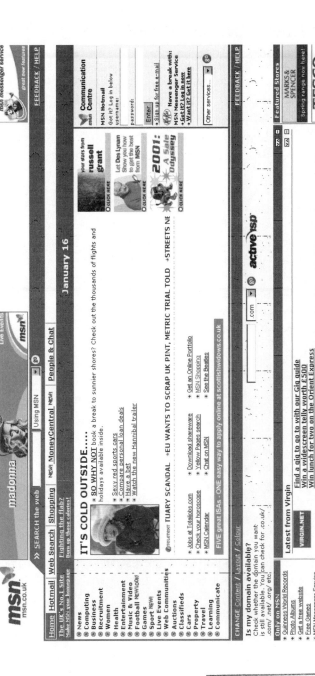

Figure 4.1 An Internet Service Provider's portal page (MSN)

FINDING AN ENGINE OR INDEX

There's something surreal about using a Web site to find a Web site – how do you find the search engine or index in the first place? Most of us find our search engines by recommendation (I can still remember the excitement when AltaVista first appeared), by reference in a magazine or book or from another site. Often the portal sites provided by ISPs and large software companies have built-in links to search engines.

Sample Sites

Search engines

Favourite search engines come and go, but these general purpose monsters will often deliver. Note that the Index sites on page 50 also have search facilities, and similarly many of these search engines now feature index 'channels' or 'categories'.

- AltaVista – www.altavista.com
- Excite – www.excite.com
- Go – www.go.com
- Google – www.google.com
- HotBot – www.hotbot.com
- Lycos – www.lycos.com
- Web Crawler – www.webcrawler.com

For further help try some of these sites whose sole purpose is to tell you about search engines:

- All in One – www.albany.net/allinone
- Beaucoup – www.beaucoup.com
- Search.com – www.search.com
- Search Engine Watch – www.searchenginewatch.com

Search engine tip: many engines have local variants. Try some of these for the UK, or look out for equivalents in other countries. However, you often don't want to limit your search to home-grown information and should always consider the US engines too.

- AltaVista – www.altavista.co.uk
- Datagold – www.datagold.com
- Excite – www.excite.co.uk
- Lycos – www.lycos.uk
- Search UK – www.searchuk.com
- UK Plus – ukplus.co.uk

SIMPLE SEARCHING

Most search engines have two ways of specifying what you want. The 'simple' approach involves typing whatever you like into a single box and letting the engine get on with it. The more complex interface often provides more ability to sharpen just what you want. It's rather like the difference between going to a restaurant and saying 'I'd like a nice pizza' or asking for 'a pizza with pepperoni and onion, except I don't want any tomato sauce'.

It makes sense to start with the simple approach, which is what you are usually faced with when you arrive at the site. Feel free to get your hands dirty with more complexity (covered in the next section), but you might as well give simplicity a chance first. Even so, there's nothing wrong with tipping the balance in your favour. Many search engines, given a list of words, will think the earlier ones are more important. Say you were looking for Austin Seven Cars. There are a lot more cars than Austins (and even more Sevens) – so by keeping the Austin up front, instead of entering Cars Austin Seven, you've a better chance of getting a good response in the first couple of pages.

Most simple searches can also handle full phrases. You might think you are always doing this, and so might be quite surprised when your request for Austin Seven Cars comes up with an item on Ferraris. In fact, a search engine generally takes each word separately, then combines the results. But you can force it to look for the exact phrase. The most common way of doing this is to enclose it in double quotes (a.k.a. inverted commas or double blips): "Austin Seven Cars". Note, by the way, that I've been using capital letters here to make it clearer in the text what it is that I'm typing. Most search engines don't care whether or not you use capitals. See the Case sensitivity Zoom in for more information.

Case sensitivity

Bearing in mind that computers have no real intelligence, it's not surprising that they think Austin and austin are two separate words. Unless you tell it differently, a computer won't recognize any similarity between 'A' and 'a'. Luckily, most search engines have been programmed for human beings, and don't distinguish between upper and lower case letters. In general, it's safest to start a search all in lower case, but experiment with capitals at the start of words if you don't get much response. Some search engines will assume that a set of words with capitals at the start makes a phrase. Such engines will treat Austin Seven Cars as if it were "austin seven cars".

In Chapter 1 we met the concept of keywords, coming up with this short list for an Austin Seven search: Austin, Seven, car, 7, automobile, vintage, veteran, chummy. It generally doesn't make sense to throw in too many items at once. Go instead for the keywords that seem to combine a unique selection with realistic content. I might start with *austin chummy*. If this failed, I could then swap various keywords around rather than throwing everything in.

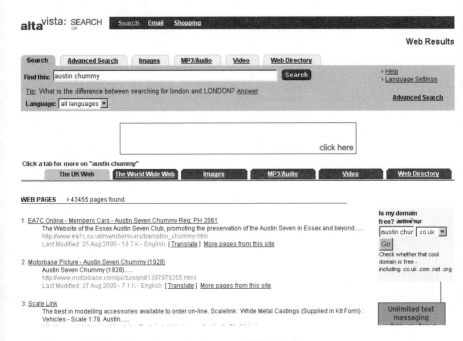

Figure 4.2 Searching for austin chummy (AltaVista)

Even fairly specific words like austin and chummy can produce many irrelevant results – in this case, there were over 43,000 responses, of which perhaps 200 were relevant. This needn't be a worry, as the search engine will attempt to put more relevant documents first (many of the later entries will just have one word matched). If it is a problem, there are ways to be more specific about what you want. We'll look at the more sophisticated search options and what to do with the results later. For now, try a few basic searches in some of the better known search engines. It would help to try a few different engines with the same search to get a feel for the way they respond (see Sample sites, Search engines above) – AltaVista makes a good starting point.

Try It

Simple searches

Experiment with a few basic searches in different engines. Feel free to make the topic whatever you like, but here are a few suggestions:

- Look up your home town;
- Look up your school or college;
- Look up a favourite TV or movie star (expect to be deluged);
- If you have a hobby, look it up;
- Look up the company you work for;
- Look up a famous historical character.

This exercise will give you some experience with the search engines themselves and also a feel for the depth of coverage on the Web. For the moment, just glance through the search results. If anything looks interesting, click on it to see what it's about. Try the different styles mentioned above – putting words in different orders, enclosing them in quotes, trying with and without capital letters.

THERE'S ENGLISH AND ENGLISH

Before we go into the deeper side of searching, it's important to remember just what you are searching in. The good news, if English is your first language, is that the majority of the Internet uses English – in fact, it's probably one of the biggest pressures towards English becoming a worldwide universal language. However, different countries employ different variants of English.

When you enter your keywords into a search engine, be aware of this. Are you using a word that has variant spellings – colour and color, centre and center? Are you thinking of something that will be described differently in another country – cars and automobiles, cinema and movies? If so, be prepared to ring the changes and try different variants on your keywords, just in case. Be prepared for some surprises too – some perfectly innocuous words in your English may have less salubrious meanings in the UK, the United States or Australia.

You also need be aware of getting spellings wrong. This can work two ways – you could spell a word wrong, and it's also possible that a Web site could have it wrong (they are, after all, written by human beings). For example if you were interested in looking back at the millennium, it wouldn't do any harm to look for millenium too.

SLICK SEARCHING

It may be that your basic search came up with just the right result. Great. But equally you could be dealing with too much or too little. We'll see more on dealing with the output later in the chapter – for the moment, let's concentrate on being more smart about what we are searching for. Time to get into expert mode. Almost all search engines allow you to go beyond a simple chunk of text as your search requirement. Some have special expert or power search screens with different boxes to control the more sophisticated searching. Pretty well all of them allow you to add some special bits of text to your search request to specify more clearly what it is that you want. In fact, we've already seen this in action when a phrase was enclosed in inverted commas.

The bad news is that different search engines have different approaches to expert searching. All the features you'll see in this section are available in some search engines, but any particular engine might lack certain capabilities, or might use a different instruction to make it happen. These are the most common, though. In these examples I have stuck to instructions which are added into the search term – the text you type into the search box. Where a search engine has a special expert screen, it will simply provide words like 'and' in little drop-down boxes to save you the effort of typing them.

Before we get into magic words, the first way of expanding your search capability is the humble star or asterisk. Let's say you wanted to look at information on electronic organs, but you knew that some types are called electric organs instead (I don't know if this is true). If you were a human being, you could scan a list looking for 'any organs beginning with electr', which would capture both types. Similarly, you can ask most search engines for words beginning with electr by typing *electr** – note there's no space between electr and the *. This is interpreted as anything beginning electr. Similarly, if you are looking for a name which begins Smith, *Smith** will get you Smith, Smithe, Smithson, Smithsonian and any other strange extension of the word you can imagine.

The next easiest control is the use of plus (+) and minus (-). Generally, when you give a search engine a list of words, it tries to match every one, but doesn't worry if it can't. If you stick a plus in front of the word (again without a space), it must appear in the document. You can do this for any or all of the words you supply. Similarly, putting a minus in front of a word will insist that that word doesn't appear in the page that is retrieved. So asking for *+pasta +green -lasagne* should result in information on green pasta that isn't lasagne. (It won't always work: you would also get a page which talked about putting pasta in a green bowl.) Note that this feature is the least common one – it is available in AltaVista and a number of other engines, but it is worth checking the search engine's help to make sure.

The final, most flexible feature is more generally available. This is often called Boolean searching, as it relies on using Boolean logic – but don't worry if this sounds painfully academic; provided you take it slowly, it all makes sense. Boolean searches use a handful of special words to link to various parts of your request. They are:

- *and* – the search engine should return only pages which have the items on both sides of the 'and' in them;
- *or* – the search engine should return pages which have either of the items on either side of the 'or' in them;
- *not* – the search engine should return pages which don't have the item that follows the 'not' in them;

■ *near* – the search engine should return only pages where the items either side of the 'near' are near each other in the page (how near is usually separately defined).

Added to these four special words, Boolean searches make use of round brackets and double quotes to link words. As we've already seen, double quotes mean that the words should be looked for as a continuous phrase, while round brackets are used to avoid ambiguity. For example, if I asked for *cats and dogs or rabbits* there are two possible meanings to my request. I could want:

■ either both cats and dogs, or just rabbits;
■ either cats and dogs, or cats and rabbits.

To make sure I meant the first, I could say *(cats and dogs) or rabbits*, while to force the second meaning I could use *cats and (dogs or rabbits)*. If this doesn't make sense, work through the phrases slowly – it's easiest to make sense if you read it aloud, leaving a gap when you hit a bracket.

Try It

Slick searching

Visit a search engine and try out the techniques above. See if there is an 'advanced' search page (or similar) and see what it offers. See what difference is made to your results if you enclose parts of the text in double blips, or use linking words like *and* and *not*.

Here's a couple more Boolean searches to help make the approach more clear: *recipe and pizza and not tomato* – will hopefully come up with a pizza recipe for those who don't like tomatoes. Some search engines will let you do without the 'and' before the 'not'. *(TV or television) and (sf or sci-fi or "science fiction") and not (x-files or xfiles)* – should provide information on TV science fiction programs (using some of the common terms for science fiction), but not the *X-Files*. Note the double blips around science fiction.

zoom in

What am I searching?

While many search engines span the Web, some allow you to choose specialist subsets or other parts of the Internet. Look out for one of those drop-down selection boxes (the ones with a line of text and a downward-pointing arrow to the right) labelled something like 'Search in'. Typical choices might be all of the Web, this site, or within the results of your previous search. We'll see more of this last choice in the 'Handling the results section' below.

Another possibility is to search newsgroups. These rambling discussions (for more details, see page 72) might seem all chat at first sight, but often you will find an insight into an important topic. Many search engines will automatically search newsgroups as well as the Web. If you are particularly interested in searching Newsgroups try this specialist site:

- Deja – www.deja.com
- Reference – www.reference.com
  (Deja is now part of google.com, but the address still works.)

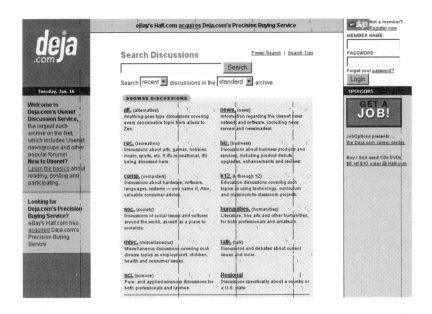

Figure 4.3 The Deja newsgroup search engine

NOT JUST ONE ENGINE

Don't despair if your first search attempt comes up with very little. The chances are that another search engine will provide more useful results. This seems particularly the case when you use the UK engines. Unfortunately, it's not possible to point to a single engine and say 'that's the best'. Most regular users have their favourite – mine's AltaVista – but it won't be best all the time. If your initial search fails, try a few different ways of expressing it. If you are still having problems, switch engine. This may seem a little tedious – if so, there are tools to use more than one search engine at once – see Chapter 5, 'Agents and ferrets', for more details. However, multi-engine searches are usually limited to using the subset of features that are common to all the engines used. For many searches, the simple action of trying one or more other engines is the best way to expand your search.

INDEXES

Search engines aren't always the best way to find something. After all, they're arbitrary and stupid. There are times when it makes more sense to look at information that has been examined and structured by real human beings. It's here that the indexes or subject catalogues (sometimes called channels or directories) come into play. So when would you want to use an index?

If you are looking for more information on a general subject, an index is a good starting point. If you want to know about Sony Corporation, there are better ways to get started, but if you want to know about the electronics industry an index will stand you in good stead. The same is true if you are totally vague about what it is you do want – working through the structured classifications of an index may well help you get you ideas together, even if you then decide to switch your allegiance to a search engine.

miners' tales

Into the index

For a later chapter I wanted to look at a good selection of software products called agents. Putting terms like *agent software* or *agent +software +internet* into a search engine produced too broad a set of results. By turning to an index, I could work down to the category Internet within Computing. I now knew that everything I might see would be about the Internet. I then searched on the word agent and came up with a good list of companies. This would only be a limited selection – remember indexes are assembled by people – but gave me everything I needed.

Indexes are arranged by categories. When you start there will be maybe 20 top-level categories like Arts or Computing. Choosing one of these brings up a lower level set of categories – so within Arts there might be Dance, Literature, Music, Painting, Sculpture, Theatre and so on. Each of these would have its own sub-categories. Eventually, by branching down through the categories, you come to a list of Web sites. These will be very selective – there is no pretence of being comprehensive – but will be very

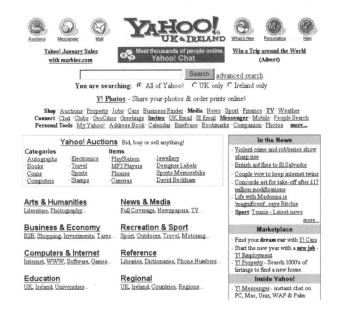

Figure 4.4 An index, showing top level categories (Yahoo!)

Try It

Indexes

Visit Yahoo! (www.yahoo.com). Try pursuing a subject of interest to you down the category chain, seeing how the details build until you hit a list of pages.

---

likely to be relevant. The better indexes allow you to stop at any level of the categories and do a search at that level.

Bear in mind, though, that indexes will be more out-of-date than a search engine, because it takes more time for a human being to examine a site and classify it than it does for an automated system.

Sample Sites

Indexes

Or subject catalogues. The distinction is getting more fuzzy, as many search engines now have some form of 'channels' or categories. The main thing to remember is that indexes are generally subject to human editorship, while search engines aren't:

- Argus Clearing House (actually an index of indexes) – clearinghouse.net
- The Librarian's Index – sunsite.berkeley.edu/internetindex
- DMOZ (Open Directory) – www.dmoz.org
- Look Smart – www.looksmart.com
- NBCi (click on Search & Find) – www.nbci.com
- Yahoo! – www.yahoo.com

Index tip: many indexes have local variants. Try some of these for the UK, or look out for equivalents in other countries. However, you often don't want to limit your search to home-grown information and should always consider the US engines too.

- MSN (Microsoft's online portal) – www.msn.co.uk
- Yahoo – www.yahoo.co.uk
- Yell – www.yell.co.uk

If you are using indexes, it's worth also looking into Web rings. These are groupings of sites on related topics. See 'Ringing the changes', page 114.

HANDLING THE RESULTS

So, you've entered your search and waited anxiously for a response. Finally the results page appears. A number of things could happen at this point. There could be nothing. No results at all. Oops. You had better check your spelling. Search engines, remember, are dumb. They aren't going to correct typing mistakes for you. If it all looks okay, throw in some of your alternative keywords (see Zoom in, Keywords – page 9). Still no luck? Make sure you've used your search engine properly (see above for obscure matters like using inverted commas and selections). Failing that, take the advice above on using more than one engine. I have regularly had a poor response, then gone to another engine that has hit the nail on the head.

The opposite can happen too. It's not exactly uncommon to see 'AltaVista found 1,317,000 Web pages for you' or something similar. This sounds a trifle overwhelming. Luckily, it is only a starting point. Check the first three pages or so of results. For simple searches, most engines will try to put the most relevant entries up front. They won't always succeed, but it's worth seeing what they've managed. If that doesn't get you anywhere, try some of your alternative keywords (see Zoom in, Keywords – page 9). Check out the 'Slick searching' section above to find out how to refine your search by adding in extra terms. Or look at some of the possibilities below for second stage searching.

Whatever you get, you will need to move from a list of responses to the information you want. Don't click everything in sight. Flick through the search engine's results looking for appropriate words. Does it look to be readable? (Even if it's in a foreign language, you may be able to read it – see 'More portal goodies' below.) Does it seem to have some relevance to what you are after? Watch out for different pages on the same site mentioned multiple times – it doesn't mean there's anything wrong with the site, but sometimes a search engine gets carried away with the number of pages it lists. Don't be too selective, though. It may be that you click through to a site that hasn't the information you need, but has lots of links to sites that do.

miners' tales

A longer list

Most search engines restrict the number of responses they put on a page to a fairly small number. This is to help people with slow connections, who don't want to wait too long for the responses to appear. If the engine returns 10 responses, I usually find it quite practical to choose more – try between 20 and 50 as a first shot. That way there's less messing about with the 'More' button.

SECOND STAGE SEARCHING

So despite your best efforts filtering the results and tuning the search, you've still got the wrong answer – or too many answers. Where do you go from here? Glance through the first couple of pages of responses. Where something seems vaguely related, scan through the actual page. Look for alternative keywords within the page. For example, if I was looking for a new telephone exchange for my business to get closer working with my computer, I might use the search term *"telephone exchange" computer*. When I glance through the results, it becomes obvious that vendors tend to refer to telephone exchanges as 'switches', and that 'computer telephony integration' or CTI is a standard term for this requirement. Using this information, I can change keywords and get a much richer response.

If, on the other hand, there are already too many possible sites listed, some of the search engines will allow you to limit a new search to the results of a previous one. That way you can add extra search terms without starting again from scratch. The different search engines have their own ways of refining a search. For example, AltaVista has both 'related searches', which suggests alternative phrases to search on that might yield a different result, and 'extend your search', which pulls in results from other services like Ask Jeeves. Other search engines like Excite let you move from a single result to the entry in the structured index that the particular result fits in, giving other, similar responses.

MORE PORTAL GOODIES

Increasingly, portal sites like search engines provide a much wider range of facilities than simple searching. It's worth spending a few minutes exploring your favourite portals to see just what they have on offer. Here's a few examples at the time of writing: practically any portal site will offer something, and the contents change all the time, so do take the time to explore.

Most sites offer free e-mail (extra e-mail addresses to those supplied by your Internet service provider, which can be accessed anywhere in the world using a Web browser), white pages (e-mail, telephone and address locators) and yellow pages. Others offer local weather, share prices and even (AltaVista) automatic translation.

Try It

Extra goodies

Visit AltaVista (www.altavista.com or www.altavista.co.uk). Click on Translate in the services list (it's under resources in the UK version). Try a few simple sentences. You might like to translate it from English to another language and back again to see what happens. You can also use this service to translate a foreign language Web page, either by entering the URL here or by clicking the word 'Translate' that crops up at the end of each item the search engine returns. Explore more of the services in AltaVista and some of the other search engines and indexes listed above.

IS IT ALL TRUE?

It's sad to relate, but not everything on the World Wide Web, or the wider Internet for that matter, is true. We could get into an esoteric philosophical discussion about the nature of truth here, but this is a practical book, so let's stick to practicalities. The Internet, and particularly the Web is great because it allows experts with very specialist knowledge to publish that knowledge to the world, but it also lets cranks and fanatics put up their own views with no magic means of determining which is which.

Before assuming that everything you read is true, give it a little thought. After all, few of us believe everything we read in a newspaper, let alone on the free-ranging Web. If you have any doubt, a starting point should be the authority of those responsible for the site. Is it produced by a respected body – a well-known encyclopedia, a university, or a respectable news source? Is there any evidence that the publisher of the site has written books on the subject, or has other ways of showing wider expertise? Sometimes a site can be both authoritative and dubious. For example, a company should be able to be authoritative (if potentially boastful) about themselves, but you have to take anything they say about competitors with a severe pinch of salt. Even when talking about their own products, there is likely to be a degree of hyperbole.

It would be a mistake, though, to ignore individually developed sites entirely, assuming that they are the work of deluded people on their electronic soapboxes. It may well be that the definitive expert on the Mongolian sand-hopper is an amateur who has given her life to the study of an insect that no university has bothered to consider. Academics can be poor sources of information on practical subjects – a businessman with real experience may well be able to write much more definitively than a professor who has spent years studying the subject. There is no magic formula for being sure here – sometimes it will come down to instinct.

COLLECTING AND REPORTING

So finally you have got hold of a range of pages which you are going to make use of. What do you do now? As we've already discovered, with a modern browser you can probably go offline and still return to the pages in question, but you are presumably undertaking this research for a purpose and now need to process the information. It's important as you follow through a Web search that you bookmark pages you may wish to return to. Do this either by putting them into a temporary bookmarks (favourites) folder, or by dragging shortcuts to your desktop. Otherwise you will find at the end of the session you have visited maybe 50 sites and can't remember which were the two that were really promising.

If you were just looking for an address or phone number it may be enough to read it off the screen. Alternatively you might like to print the page to get a hard copy of the results. Bear in mind that many Web pages are divided up into separate frames – this is the case, for example, when there's a bit of the screen down the left which doesn't scroll as you scroll the right hand side up and down. Some browsers don't handle printing of frames very well – with a modern browser you should be able to choose what you get, but bear this in mind before trying to print 50 pages' worth of output.

If you intend to combine the results of several sites, you may find it helpful to cut and paste pages into a word processor. Web browsers aren't quite as good at selecting text to copy as some programs, but with a little fiddling you should be able to highlight the appropriate section and paste it elsewhere. Many word processors will even keep the formatting for you.

When it comes to pictures, you may want to handle them a little differently. For Windows users, there's a neat facility in Navigator and Internet Explorer which allows you to right-click a picture, then choose to use it as your backdrop. Any of the main browsers will let you save the picture file to your PC – usually it will have an obscure name given to it by the Web site's developer. You may like to change this to something more meaningful to you.

If you do intend to do something with the results other than just read them (for instance, include them in a report or an item for publication), bear in mind the restrictions of copyright. Everything on the Web is copyright, though some items might be specifically marked as available for general copying. See page 121 for more details.

RECAP

Portal sites like an ISP's page, a search engine or an index provide a structured way into the Web. Often well-chosen keywords will be enough to find what you are looking for with a search engine, but sometimes you will need to use more sophisticated tools, like Boolean searches. Indexes provide an alternative to search engines, with less content but more human guidance and structure. They tend to be better if you are looking for a type of thing, rather than a specific thing.

Sometimes the initial results of a search will need refinement – by changing the keywords, or using the special features of the search engine. If this still doesn't help, trying different engines is worthwhile.

5 SKILLS
Agents and ferrets

> ■ Pulling together search results from several places;
> ■ Special search engines;
> ■ Clever software;
> ■ Adding search features into the browser.

I WANT IT ALL

In looking at search engines, we found that different engines came up with very different results. Sometimes you might end up trawling through half a dozen different engines. At some point, the realization is liable to strike that you are doing something rather strange. After all, the Internet is all about connecting different computers and programs – how come it's you that is having to do all the work?

This chapter is about getting help with search engines. Instead of trying one after another, wouldn't it be handy if there was a computer program to do it for you? The good news is that there are such programs – in fact several different types. The bad news (isn't there always bad news?) is that taking such an approach isn't entirely trivial. It usually takes longer than a simple search, and any computer program which is set up to get between you and another program may make mistakes. It may simply be programmed wrong. It could have out-of-date information about how search engines work. Or, bearing in mind the different ways search engines ask for information, it may have to resort to using the most basic features that are common to all the engines you choose to use.

The bad news means that you can't adopt this approach all the time. But it's a great starting point for a piece of in-depth research – you can always use search engines directly afterwards to refine a particular aspect. Broadly, approaches to super-searches can be divided into four: meta-searching, ferrets, agents and browser search facilities.

META-SEARCHING

A meta-search engine is one that gets results from multiple sources. Some such engines offer extra features – Ask Jeeves tries to answer a question in English, while Quickbrowse can link together entire Web pages to give a result that has everything you need in one place.

To avoid being overwhelmed with response, meta-search engines also limit how much reply they take. You may have some way of varying this, but at least be aware of it. You won't always want to use a meta-search engine, but if you have a difficult requirement, or aren't having any luck with your favourite sources, it's worth giving one a try.

Sample Sites

Meta-search engines

Hit a good range of other engines with these front-ends.

- Ask Jeeves – www.ask.com or www.ask.co.uk
- Dogpile – www.dogpile.com
- Internet Sleuth – www.isleuth.com
- Metacrawler – www.metacrawler.com
- Quickbrowse – www.quickbrowse.com
- Search.com – www.search.com

Figure 5.1 A meta-search engine (Dogpile)

FERRETS

I ought to say straight off that 'ferrets' isn't an accepted terminology for this sort of search facility – but it ought to be. Where meta-searching involves getting one Web search engine to query a number of others, a ferret is a piece of software running on your PC that knows a bit about search engines. So, you put your subject into the ferret and it runs off to a number of engines and pumps the topic in.

Because of the way the Internet works, this is not quite as time-consuming as it sounds. Although you may only do one thing at a time, the ferret can set up several queries without waiting for the responses. Up to now, the results aren't that different from a meta-search. The ferret will pull together the responses into a combined list, so you don't have to flit between the different search engines to see what they found. But the particularly nice thing is that this is only the beginning.

What many products then do is visit each site that came from the search engine, make sure it's actually there (remember search engines' entries are often out-of-date), and tries to summarize its contents for you. All the results of doing this are available offline for you to study. Want more depth? You can just click on an item to visit the page, which will often remain cached on your PC, and even if it doesn't, only involves a quick connection to download it.

Obviously there is a price for this extra service. It takes time to connect to each page and summarize the contents. In theory this could be horrendous. If your search subject threw up hundreds of thousands of sites, you could have a very long wait. Luckily, ferrets give up on a site if it takes too long to emerge, and they will only usually consider the first one or two pages of search engine results, limiting the entries to a manageable size.

Sample Sites

Ferrets

There are a good number of products available to perform this task. I have to mention Web Ferret, if only because of the name and because the basic version is free. Software dates just as quickly as Web addresses, but at the time of writing, it would be worth trying one of these sites:

- Bullseye – www.intelliseek.com
- Copernic – www.copernic.com
- Infoseek Express – express.infoseek.com
- Web Inspector – www.ari.de/english
- Web Ferret – www.ferretsoft.com
- Web Sleuth – www.imsi.co.uk

If they've become out-of-date, try searching for 'search managers', or 'web search managers' or 'search utilities' in a search engine or index.

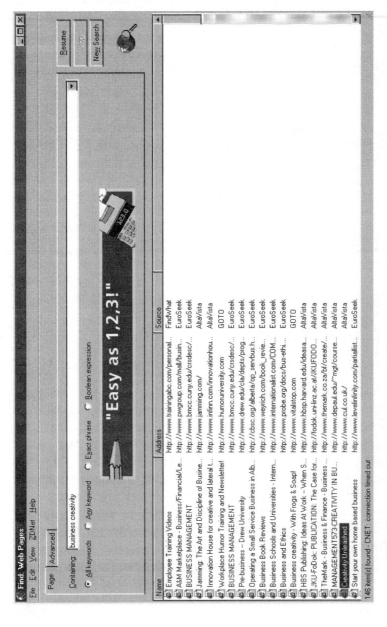

Figure 5.2 A ferret's search results (Web Ferret)

SENSIBLE FERRETING ABOUT

A ferret will usually return a fairly long list of references. You can take a few quick actions to make them more manageable. First have a weeding pass. There will be some entries that are utterly irrelevant to your requirements. They might be advertising screens you always get from the search engine. They might be pages that simply don't exist, or are clearly irrelevant. If the ferret timed out while trying to get hold of them, and the page sounds interesting, you might like to retry it (most ferrets have a mechanism for doing this).

After deleting the definitely irrelevant entries, make a positive pass. Look for entries where the summary seems relevant. Ferrets tend to summarize by picking out keywords or section starts. Glancing through this text will often be enough to know whether or not a site is likely to give more information that's of value. At this stage, you can either flag up the pages for further reference (if the ferret doesn't have a facility to do this, you could delete all the rest), or visit them as you go. In a surprisingly short time, you should have a good selection of information.

BRANCHING OUT

Some pages provide valuable links to other pages. As you scan through the summaries in your ferret results, this should be obvious. Ferrets often list number of links out from the page, and even if yours doesn't, the page's title and summary should give it away. When you see a links page, try to identify whether these are links that are directly relevant to your topic. You may need to glance at the page itself to confirm this. If they are, most ferrets have a facility to add to its list all the pages pointed to by a particular page. As a first search quite often doesn't come up with the exact result you want, but may provide a page that is linked to something appropriate, this is extremely valuable.

Obviously the law of diminishing returns comes into play, but you may make several levels of excursions along links, each time pulling in extra links from a newly found page. This way you are getting over the fallibility of the automatic processes used by the original search engine by making use of collections of links made by human beings who are knowledgeable about the topic. In a few iterations, your pool of sources on the subject can be hugely increased.

AGENTS

Agents are subtle variants on ferrets – in fact sometimes so subtle that the only distinction is a fancier user interface. The idea of an agent is that it's a piece of software that performs a task on your behalf, as if it were a person. This means that ferrets are agents really, but not very clever ones.

Agent technology isn't particularly well developed at the moment, but the distinction I am making is that a ferret is simply a piece of software running on your PC that happens to be connected to the Web. An agent is more independent. You set an agent going on a problem in a very similar way, but then you should be able to disconnect from the Internet. When at a later date you connect up, it should either send you an e-mail or wait for you to summon it – in either case, it should then present back the information it has collected.

Of course, an agent is a very attractive concept if you are paying for your connection time to the Internet. There's also something rather exciting about the concept of an agent as an independent entity that is zooming around the Web on your behalf. In reality, there's something different happening. An agent is a ferret in wolf's clothing. It manages its trick, because it is based on another computer, usually one that is connected to the Internet all the time. When you start an agent going, it actually starts a ferret-like task on this other computer. When it has assembled the information it either mails them to you, or holds them until you come looking for them.

Sample Sites

Agents

At the time of writing, agents are still in the early stages of development. There a few sites listed below. To find the latest developments look in Yahoo! or another index. Go down the index to 'internet' or 'computers and internet' then search within that

---

category for 'agent'.

- Agent Web – agents.umbc.edu – not a manufacturer but a great source of information on agents
- Autonomy – www.autonomy.com
- Gossip – www.tryllian.com

Companies who make agents don't do it out of the kindness of their corporate hearts. Unlike a normal portal site, they can't rely on advertising to support their venture. Instead, they will usually charge you for the privilege of using their agent. But you have to weigh that charge up against the savings you will make on connection charges. Note that most agent software will also act as a ferret – check the vendors for details.

BROWSER SEARCH FACILITIES

The latest versions of the top browsers have built-in features to help with searching – and you can stretch them even further by adding in specialist search assistants. Internet Explorer features a Search button, which brings up a side bar in which a search can be entered and fed sequentially to a number of preset search pages. More interesting though, is the related button. Clicking on Customize in the Toolbars section of the View menu will enable you to add new buttons. Select the Related button. Now when you navigate to a page, then click the related button, a side bar will open with suggestions for similar pages you may want to visit.

In Navigator, both a similar Related tab and a Search tab appears in the standard side bar. Though the Related feature appears to work by magic, it is using the keywords that are built into most Web sites to find similar links. Both products used a cut down version of the Alexa product (see below). A number of search engines, such as Lycos, also provide quick ways to add extra search functionality to your browser at their sites.

┌───┐
│   **Sample Sites**   │
├───┤
│   │
│   **Browser search facilities**   │
│   │
│ These products will improve your search capabilities │
│ from within your browser.   │
│   │
│ ■ Alexa – www.alexa.com – more sophisticated   │
│   version of the built-in related feature   │
│ ■ Excite Assistant – www.excite.com/assist/html/   │
│   download – search toolbar linked to Excite   │
│ ■ Lycos See More – www.lycos.com/seemore – right-   │
│   click any word on a page to look in up in Lycos   │
│ ■ Yahoo Companion – edit.yahoo.com/config/   │
│   download_companion   │
│   │
└───┘

RECAP

A single search engine won't always deliver, while a meta-search engine allows you to cover a number of different sources. The price you pay is only coping with simple searches. Alternatively you can use special software – ferrets or agents – which will manage the search process for you.

If you would like to build more search capabilities into your browser, features like Alexa's related information can make it easier to springboard off to similar pages.

6 SKILLS

Information from people

- ■ Involving other people;
- ■ Using e-mail;
- ■ Newsgroups and conferences;
- ■ Chatting online.

GETTING PEOPLE INVOLVED

The Internet is not just a broadcast medium like TV – it's a communication medium, which means you can not only search for information, but actually ask real people for help. Bear in mind, if you adopt this strategy, that 'real people' bit. The people who might answer your query aren't just a presence in an electronic directory. They've got their own life, their own business, their own time to deal with. Your problems aren't their problems.

To try to get this position in perspective, few of us would walk up to a complete stranger in the street and ask them for anything more than the time or directions. Similarly, most Internet contacts will respond more favourably if you ask something that can be answered quickly, without going off and looking something up.

E-MAIL – GETTING A REPLY

The most direct approach is e-mail. If you have someone's e-mail address, you can ask that person for help. Be very careful how you do this. The chances of getting a worthwhile reply depend crucially on how you word a request for help. Here are five top tips for getting a response:

1. *Personalize* – don't make it look as if you are sending your request to 100 people, even if you are. Address your e-mails individually, and make sure there is some personalization in the message. Lots of people ignore circulars.
2. *Be concise* – your e-mail will be vying for attention with others in the in-box. If it's clear and to the point, without being over-lengthy, it is more likely to be read and acted on.
3. *Choose a topic that the person is likely to be interested in* – most of us are so enthusiastic about our interests that we will spend time discussing them with complete strangers. Make use of this tendency, and also demonstrate your own interest in the area, making you a fellow enthusiast.
4. *Offer something in return* – you may well have your own areas of expertise. Knowledge is a great commodity for bartering. By saying 'and if you ever need anything on X, just let me know', you are turning your request for information into a trade. Remember to follow through, though, if someone takes you up.
5. *Give a clear context* – make it obvious why you are asking. Some people are a bit suspicious of a straight question out of the blue. If you say what you do and how you intend to use the information (subject to tip 2), your request is more attractive. The one proviso to this is some people are wary of particular groups (for example, students or big business) – if there's an obvious potential for irritation, be careful what you say.

These tips won't necessarily get you a reply. Many people have a policy of ignoring unsolicited mail. Others, like Bill Gates or the Queen, get so much mail that it's impossible to reply personally – and you may get a message to that effect. In fact, if you are 'cold mailing' you must expect the majority of your attempts to fail – but the approach can be well worth it for the odd occasion when it is successful.

A cold mail that worked

This e-mail to my Web site got a favourable and hopefully helpful reply (though accompanied by a warning that the approach wouldn't work again). The fact that someone had taken the initiative to contact me (because *Fahrenheit 451* was in my online bookshop) interested me enough to reply. The student scored on four out of five of the top tips above.

Hello, I am a tenth-grade student at Cliffside Park High School in Cliffside Park, New Jersey. Well, I've assigned to do a term paper on *Fahrenheit 451*. Now, I know that you don't do term papers or support people with term papers, I am fine with that, and I wasn't going to ask that anyways.

What I would like to know (if it's not too much trouble) is a main topic in the book. I read the book, and came up with 'how society gets around the government or how they break the law'. For our term paper we have to have eight full pages on that one topic. (In my opinion it's too much for a tenth-grade class, but that is what our teacher wants.) Also our teacher stresses that the term paper isn't supposed to be a synopsis of the book, all the eight pages have to be on that one subject. So, my question is: 'Is this a good enough topic, to come up with eight pages for a term paper?' If so, or if not, please e-mail me back with a reply, or a new topic, or whatever information you can provide.

THANK YOU VERY MUCH

E-MAIL – FINDING AN ADDRESS

Before you get someone to reply to you, you have to find an address in the first place. Although there isn't a single guaranteed source, there is a huge range of possibilities for digging up an appropriate address.

Sometimes, the best approach is to move away from the Internet. Increasingly, e-mail addresses are published in books, magazines and newspapers, or given out in the broadcast media. This is a good way to support tip 3 – many people who write on a topic are genuinely interested in it, and prepared to discuss it and give out information to others. If you find someone writing about keeping fancy fowl in *Chicken Breeding Monthly*, the chances are pretty high that they will help you out with a query about looking after Transylvanian Bare Necks. Even for a general question (see Miners' tales – Who's who below), they may be prepared to help.

There are no guarantees here. I write for a popular computing magazine that carries the e-mail addresses of all its contributors. I try to reply to all the e-mails I get (though of course I can't always answer a question), but I know of other contributors who never bother to respond. You are probably even more likely to get a reply if the author of a book includes an e-mail address – writers often put a lot of themselves into a book, and feel more of an obligation to communicate with their readers (who, after all, have paid money for what they have written), provided the query meets the tips I mentioned above.

Who's who

I had to get comments on creativity from a wide range of people for a book I was writing. One source I tried was the venerable publication *Who's Who*. When I tried it out it didn't carry many e-mail addresses (around 150), but there are more every year. As I was using the CD ROM version, I could search for entries with e-mail addresses to write to. Out of the 150, around 15 were appropriate. From these I got three replies, including a Nobel prize winner and the chairman of a sizeable company. Not a huge volume, but valuable input from sources which would otherwise have been unavailable.

Another good source of e-mail addresses is Web sites. You would normally think of a Web site as a direct source of information, but nearly every site also carries e-mail addresses, which can be used to get further information. Be a little careful here. With a commercial site, you won't generally want the 'Web master' or similarly titled individual (unless you want to ask how he or she managed that particularly clever effect on the home page). Instead look for individuals who are involved with the content of the site. Where possible, find an e-mail address which has a person's name, rather than a generic address like 'info@website.com' – you are more likely to get attention by someone who knows the subject.

Although corporate sites will often come up with an answer, it may well be useless PR speak, rather than valuable information. However, personal and small company sites are almost always about a subject that interests the owner. E-mail the right person with the right query and you'll probably get more material than you know what to do with.

Later on in this chapter, we will be looking at newsgroups, the online discussions that act like electronic bulletin boards where anyone can post a comment. These are great ways of tracking down someone who has a strong interest in a subject, and hence maximizing the chances of an effective reply. Because posting a message to a newsgroup automatically includes an e-mail address, you can usually send a mail to anyone who has contributed to a board. By watching the type of contributions made, you can make sure you are asking the right person. Note that there are two distinct possibilities here: sending an e-mail to an individual or posting a query in the newsgroup. We'll look at newsgroup posting in a little while.

A final possibility is to use a white pages service to look up an e-mail address (see page 100). As many white pages services give people the opportunity to list interests and special areas in their details, it is sometimes possible to search for appropriate addresses. Otherwise, this is something of a needle in a haystack approach, as it's not obvious just what you are going to look for in the directory.

Try It

Collecting addresses

Spend half an hour trying to find some useful e-mail addresses for a topic you are currently involved with. Try appropriate Web sites, magazines, books – anything that might give you a lead.

E-MAIL – WARM CALLS

Up to now we have only considered e-mail as a way of doing 'cold calls' – of contacting people you don't know. A much more productive approach is to contact people you do know. This isn't much use unless you know people with some knowledge of the subject you are interested in. While this won't always be the case, it certainly won't always be untrue either.

An essential resource for making such 'warm calls' is a good address book, stuffed full with the people you have met and corresponded with.

Generally, knowledge management professionals, who spend all their time worrying about how best to handle information, are sceptical about information squirrels. They point out that you end up with an unmanageable mass of unreliable data. You need to make a special case for the electronic address book, though. It doesn't get overfull or overwhelmed with crossing out like its paper equivalent. It just goes on growing in usefulness.

Whenever you have a contact with someone through business or your social life where e-mail addresses are exchanged, get the details into your online address book. If you then need help on a subject, you should be able to call up appropriate addressees very quickly. Of course it is going to get out-of-date, but at worst your e-mails will bounce back undelivered – you aren't wasting money by amassing extra addressees like you are with ordinary mail.

miners' tales

The little black book

I have had many valuable snippets of information from others thanks to a well-stuffed electronic address book. There are some individuals who I am always asking for help (and who reciprocate by asking me). Others are more of a one-off source when a particular subject comes up.

Recent examples have included asking a university professor who I met at a seminar for some information (she passed me on to another lecturer at a different university, who gave me everything I needed) and asking an old college friend who is now a well-regarded geophysicist for advice on a matter involving physics. The more you can maintain and support your personal network of contacts, the better the chance that they will help out with a request.

IMPERSONAL E-MAIL – MAILING LISTS

You've probably already learned to hate one form of mailing list: the ones that generate all those irritating unsolicited messages offering you a holiday of a lifetime in Florida, or naughty videos from Russia. Luckily, there's also a helpful, voluntary form of mailing list. In fact it's a half-way house between e-mail and newsgroups (see next section). Instead of sending an e-mail message to an individual or putting it up on a bulletin board for everyone to see, a mailing list (often called a list server after the mechanism for distributing the mail) lets you send a mail to one place and have it forwarded to a whole group of people interested in the same topic.

If there's a subject you have a regular interest in, a mailing list is worth joining, as you should receive useful mail on topics of interest. It's a more dangerous place to actually ask questions – most mailing list subscribers don't want to be bombarded with questions, but it's a great way of picking up background information.

One word of warning if you do use mailing lists – lists are normally joined and left by e-mail. Make sure you use the correct format and address for doing this: you don't want everyone on the list to get a copy of your request to unsubscribe.

Sample Sites

Mailing lists

Most of the mailing lists I have come across have been by personal recommendation, or from remarks in newsgroup discussions. If you want to go out and find one, there are a number of directories, including:

- www.lsoft.com/lists/list_q.html
- www.liszt.com
- tile.net/lists

Many mailing lists are managed by a few large providers. Try:

- E-groups – www.egroups.com
- Listbot – www.listbot.com

NEWSGROUPS

Newsgroups are a very different environment from the Web. Each newsgroup is, in effect, a bulletin board that anyone can send an e-mail to. The message then appears on the board for everyone to see. Conversations on the board are 'threaded', so you can see that a particular message is a reply to a previously posted one. Newsgroups exist on thousands of topics. There are particular groups, for example, for practically every type of hand-held computer in existence, or for pictures of Doctor Who. They are grouped into a handful of categories – see the Zoom in Finding the right newsgroup. You will occasionally see the term Usenet bandied about – it describes the popular public newsgroups you will find described everywhere. There are also private newsgroups run by various companies, which are not part of Usenet.

Finding the right newsgroup

Given that there are more than 50,000 newsgroups, it may not seem trivial to find the right one for your subject. One approach is to search the newsgroups – see the recommendations on page 47. Alternatively, you can make use of the newsgroup structure.

Newsgroups are structured under a range of top-level headings. You may find appropriate groups within a heading that suits your topic. Note that newsgroups are handled rather differently to the Web. Instead of providing access to a single server, your Internet service provider keeps their own copy of newsgroups, propagating updates around the Web. This means they can choose not to carry particular newsgroups, and often do so.

- alt – the alternative newsgroups. This is where all nastier groups appear, but also the cult specialities;
- biz – business subjects (strong US bias);
- comp – computing. Everything from specific hardware to general topics;
- misc – anything that doesn't appear elsewhere (except under alt!);
- rec – sports, hobbies, games and everything recreational;
- sci – science;
- soc – social, cultural, religion and anthropology.

There are also country-oriented newsgroups – for example, there are many with the top level heading UK. A final possibility is to guess at keywords. Many newsreaders, including the Outlook Express reader that comes free with Windows, allow you to type in a word, and will then pick out any newsgroups with this word in the title. Of course, you have to guess the appropriate keyword, which won't always be easy,

zoom in

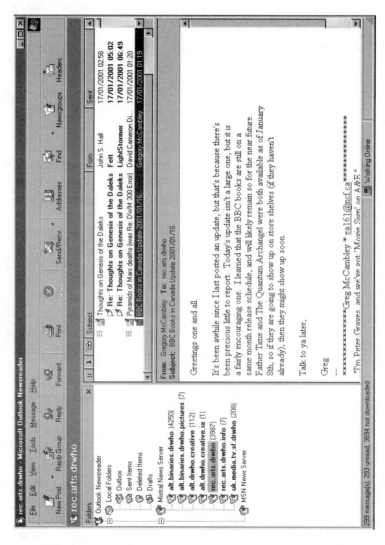

Figure 6.1 Researching via a newsgroup

but by trying a few different ones, you may well hit an appropriate group. Don't forget contractions – for example, the *Doctor Who* newsgroups all use the keyword *drwho*.

We have already met the newsgroup as a source of e-mail addresses. Newsgroups are also a great way of picking expert brains. However, you do have to go about this a little carefully. You don't get anywhere by stomping in and demanding service. A picture is helpful to understand just what is going on in a newsgroup. Imagine you wanted to find out more about clog dancing in Lancashire. You might discover that there was a Lancastrian Clog Dancing Society that met in Burnley every Friday night. If you charged in half way through a meeting, interrupted the speaker and demanded they tell you everything there was to know about the history of clog dancing, you shouldn't be surprised if you got a rather poor reception.

The same is true of a newsgroup. It is typically frequented by a group of regulars. These are people with an interest in the subject, who might have been discussing it this way for years. Being long established may make their discussion rather impenetrable to begin with. This is not helped by the ephemeral nature of the newsgroup. Messages ('postings') only stay up for a few days. To begin with you will see the tail ends of conversations without any idea of how they started. Give it a little time, visiting at least once a day so you can literally pick up the threads of what is going on. Look out for the magic term FAQ (frequently asked questions). Many newsgroups will have the most commonly asked questions tucked away somewhere. This way, they don't get asked the same thing every day. Check that the help you require isn't already there – see the Zoom in below on how to find FAQs. Watch the conversations for a while before contributing anything. Don't worry – you can't be seen while 'lurking' in this way. Get a feel for the way questions are asked and dealt with, and try to fit with the style of the newsgroup.

Frequently asked questions

zoom in

Avoid the wrath of peevish newsgroup contributors by not asking the same question that has been asked every Wednesday for the last two years. You can find FAQs by using one of the newsgroup search facilities detailed on page 47 (remember to include FAQ as a search keyword – this is a universally understood term). FAQs usually get re-posted to a newsgroup every few weeks. It's also worth simply searching the newsgroups for your question to see if someone has already answered it. Failing that, there is a FAQ archive at:

■ www.faqs.org

with a simple search routine that is well worth checking. You could also check the newsgroup news.answers which is home to a whole collection of FAQs.

When you are ready, make your query short, to the point and polite. Try to put a (very) short version of what the question is in the subject line. Don't say 'Help!!!!' – a lot of people won't bother to read your message. You are much more likely to get a response with 'How did clog dancing start?' Be particularly careful that you address your query to the right newsgroup. Newsgroup regulars are very touchy about spamming – sending an item to many newsgroups simultaneously. If they suspect this is happening, you may get some unpleasant replies.

Once you have posted your query, it's a good idea to keep an eye on the newsgroup regularly for a few days. Otherwise, because of the quick turnover, it's easy to miss any replies. If you get a response, only reply on the newsgroup if what you have to say might be of general interest. If you just want to thank someone for the information (which is a good thing to do), it's best to e-mail them directly. Third party politeness loses its appeal after a few hundred messages.

WEB CONFERENCES

While newsgroups are the slickest way to enter into online conversations, Web technology does allow for discussion too. Web conferences provide exactly the same sort of facilities as newsgroups, but they are flashier and significantly slower to display. The advantage is that you can read and contribute without ever leaving the comfort of your Web browser.

Like newsgroups, Web conferences cover practically every topic you can think of – but unlike newsgroups, they aren't all in one place. Often you'll find a conference (or discussion) as part of a Web site. So you might find that a film star's site has a conference for fans to discuss their favourite screen idol. You'll also find some more general conferences at sites dedicated to this type of discussion. If your ISP has a sizeable online presence, they too may have conferences available from their home page. MSN, for example, hosts a wide range of online discussions with regular celebrity contributors.

Sample Sites

Web conferences

You will find conferences at many specialist sites. These sites cover wider topics:

- Delphi – www.delphi.com
- EzBoard – www.ezboard.com
- Inside the Web – www.insidetheweb.com
- iVillage – www.ivillage.com – wide-ranging boards on women's issues

UK

- iVillage – www.ivillage.co.uk – wide-ranging boards on women's issues

Or get an overview of many discussion sites in the online communities index at:

- Forum One – www.forumone.com

CHAT

Communication via the Internet does not have to have the indirect feel of e-mail or newsgroups – it's possible to use the Internet to make a direct connection. This can be by typing – the ubiquitous 'Chat' – or even voice or video. You can't include Internet communication mechanisms without including Chat, though it is the least likely means of getting the information you want. Chat comes in four flavours:

- IRC (Internet Relay Chat) the basic Internet facility;

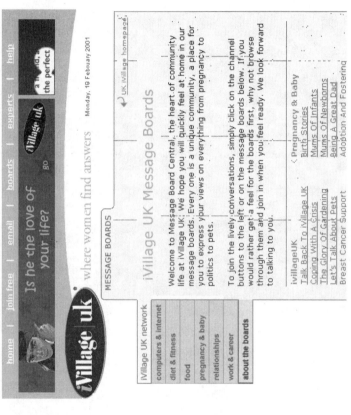

Figure 6.2 Web conferences (bulletin boards) on the iVillage women's discussion site

- avatar chat, where you are represented by a character in a virtual world;
- voice chat, going beyond typing to real speech; and
- the proprietary chat systems that are operated by some of the bigger Internet service providers.

Chat is a misleading name (except in the case of voice chat). Chat services usually enable two or more people to type information on their screen, which appears pretty well immediately on the other people's screens. The conversation appears as a series of lines of text, prefixed by some identifier, often a nickname, showing who is 'talking'.

The best known of the proprietary offerings is AOL's chat room service. Generally thought to be the main reason for AOL's success, there are thousands of chat rooms within the AOL environment, divided by various types of interest. However, it has often been said that there is only one real driver for this form of chat – sex. Not that chat rooms are necessarily used to pick up a date (some are very tightly policed), but that their reason for existing comes down to providing a mechanism for interacting safely with the opposite sex (or at least apparently opposite – you can't, of course, determine the sex of the person on the other keyboard). This driving force sadly means that a lot of chat is mindless, full of slang and of little value to the outsider. Not all chat is like this – there are sessions that focus on a specified topic, or involve discussion with a special guest (often arranged by a third party like an ISP or a broadcaster) – but much of it is worthless to the researcher.

Internet Relay Chat is much the same as AOL chat, but with less structure. Microsoft has a product that sits on top of IRC, providing cartoon-like illustrations of what the people involved are feeling. This can be fun, but you ought to make sure that you limit use of it to a comic chat server, or everyone else will get lots of irrelevant text appearing in their conversation – and tolerance levels in chat sessions are often not very high. To get going with IRC you need chat software (you may well have the Microsoft software with your web browser, and you can disable the cartoons) and a server to connect to. The site www.irchelp.org has IRC software and a big list of servers you can connect to.

If you want fancy graphics, you might be better off with one of the graphical chat worlds. These are separate services, which you often pay to be involved in. You then wander around a complex world, not unlike an adventure game, with on-screen graphics showing the world. Some actually are games, others just an environment, but in either case, most or all of the other characters are real people, who you can converse with as if you were using Chat, usually in speech bubbles. You can usually design your own character (an avatar, which is something of a misnomer if you look into the origins of the word) to reflect how you want to be in this virtual world.

One of the more interesting chat developments is voice chat or Internet telephones. You can use such facilities (the software will usually be bundled free with your browser) given a sound card to hold one-to-one calls across the Internet, but you can also link into directories to try to pull in several people with common interests. The conversations can be quite rich, as voice is supported by conventional typed chat, shared whiteboards (simple drawing/graphics packages which everyone in the conversation shares) or sharing documents. However, the Internet is relatively slow and works in chopped up packages of information, so the quality of connection is not always good. Even so, increasing connection speeds and compression of information means these direct connections are getting ever better, with the appealing possibility of having conversations anywhere in the world for the cost of a local call. In fact, the compression is getting so good that it is even possible to have a video link this way, though the quality so far is extremely poor.

YOUR OWN SITE

If you have your own Web site, you may be able to use it get information from others. Many ISPs include some free Web space as part of the deal – or you may have a business Web site that you can use. Of course, you may not get any answers this way – but it doesn't do any harm to try. This isn't the place to learn how to build a Web site. There are plenty of good books on the subject, and the Appendix to this book gives guidance on getting on to the Internet.

This sort of approach is most useful when you want to build up a background level of information – like a slow survey. You can ask visitors to your site simply to send you an e-mail on the subject, or you can give them a form to fill in. In either case, though, there needs to be a carrot.

People generally come to Web sites to find something out or to get something, not to give you something. If your Web site has lots of helpful information on a subject you are more likely to get a contribution. For example, if you want to research your surname, a good way to do it is to build a Web site with as much information as you've already gathered about your name, then to ask for further information. The sorts of people who are likely to provide information are the ones who'll be interested in seeing your site in the first place. They may also appreciate that their contribution will be itself added to the site – preferably with some acknowledgement. You might also offer to keep contributors up-to-date with new information, so by contributing something they get back other facts on a subject of interest.

RECAP

The Internet is a communication vehicle that can reach millions of people. If used correctly, this is an immense resource to help with your researches. E-mail can be effective if well focused, whether using an address you have picked up from the Web or a magazine, or mailing a known contact. Newsgroups, another key source, provide online discussion points on a host of topics. Provided they are approached correctly, including consulting FAQs, newsgroups are an excellent source of information.

7 FOCUS

Quick reference and news

- **Looking for a specific fact;**
- **The best of the news;**
- **Weather too.**

THE WORLD'S LARGEST ENCYCLOPEDIA?

When I was young, my parents bought a 20-volume encyclopedia, mostly justifying it because it would be a valuable asset in my education. Like all encyclopedias, it had its limitations, but it was very good if you just wanted to find out a fact – in fact one volume even had a sort of 'fact book' in it. But it was bulky, expensive and slow to use. Today, the CD ROM has made encyclopaedias much more accessible. If you need a particular piece of information, a CD ROM encyclopedia is probably the best starting point. It's immediately available (well, as soon as your PC has started up) and is very quick and easy to search.

Unfortunately it is also limited. Firstly it gets out-of-date. Many CD ROM encyclopedias have mechanisms for getting monthly updates, but these usually only last a year, and tend to be more about current events than updating facts. More significantly, despite its huge capacity, a CD ROM is minuscule in Internet terms. While there is a whole lot of stuff in there, plenty more facts simply aren't covered. You need a bigger encyclopedia. Like the Web.

As usual, things aren't quite as easy as we wish they would be. Unless you've skipped Chapter 4, you have already seen how searching the Web isn't always simple. The same goes for finding facts – because you aren't actually looking in an encyclopedia, but rather a vast, disordered library (remember the image of fishing around in a huge building, where people are constantly throwing new books through the window). What you need is a site dedicated to facts, rather than trawling through the whole messy Web. Luckily, there are some.

BASIC FACTS

When it comes down to it, encyclopedias and dictionaries are the most sensible way to look up a basic fact. If you need to know the year Rome invaded Britain, the chemical symbol for lead, the meaning of syllogism or a quick quote on the subject of taxidermy, you could spend a long time working through search engine results, only to find an entry that has been mistyped. But you would be much more sensible turning to a reference book.

If your own reference materials have failed, the Web has the makings of a good reference library scattered around in different locations. Finding these sites can be a mix of intent and accident. If you come across the sort of site you are liable to make significant use of, make sure you add it to your favourites (bookmark it). Apart from the suggestions below, try looking under reference in one of the indexes – see page 49.

WHAT'S HAPPENING?

If you are interested in what's going on in the world, the Internet ought to be a good place to look. There is an immediacy about the Internet (and specifically the Web) that particularly suits news. News on the Web is a strange mix of newspaper and TV-style coverage. When done properly, it can both provide handy headlines and the sort of in-depth coverage that the other media only dream of. A real advantage for the news consumer is that you can take it all in at a high level, and just drill down to the detail of the stories which interest you most. That way you can get the coverage of a quality newspaper without having to wade through an inch-thick pile of paper.

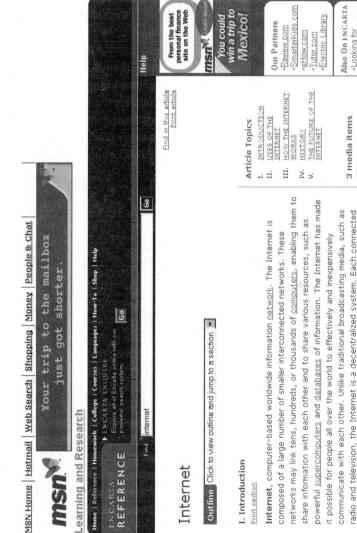

Figure 7.1 An online encyclopedia (Microsoft Encarta)

Sample Sites

Quick reference

For general reference information with many different books online:

- Internet Public Library – www.ipl.org/ref
- Virtual Reference Desk – thorplus.lib.purdue.edu/reference

Dictionaries/Thesauruses:

- Encarta World English Dictionary – dictionary.msn.com
- Merriam Webster – www.m-w.com
- One Look (links to many different dictionaries) – www.onelook.com
- Oxford English Dictionary – www.oed.com – the world's greatest English dictionary, but substantial subscription.
- Roget's Thesaurus – www.thesaurus.com

Quotations:

- Bartlett's – www.cc.columbia.edu/acis/bartleby/bartlett
- Quoteland – www.quoteland.com
- Quoteworld – www.quoteworld.org

Encyclopedias:

- Britannica – www.britannica.com
- Concise Columbia Encyclopedia – www.encyclopedia.com
- Encarta Concise Encyclopedia – encarta.msn.com

If you want to find the Samuel Johnson quote about London referred to on page 9, try in Bartlett's quotations, either under London or Samuel Johnson.

Another advantage of getting news from the Web is the worldwide flavour. Like it or not, the news you receive through the conventional media will be filtered by your own country's social and political inclinations. As more and more issues echo across Europe or have implications both sides of the Atlantic or Pacific, it's eye-opening to see the news from another viewpoint. The Internet is not only a rich way of getting information, it's a truly international one.

Virtual papers

Reading a newspaper is something of a ritual. It's a relaxation, or a way to spend some time on the train or bus. In fact, it's the antithesis of the Web. But that doesn't mean that the Web and newspapers don't go together. A newspaper Web site will often allow you to search across many issues, or to pull together stories of particular interest to you. There is so much news on the Web that you might not want to use your regular newspaper's site – it may well be more informative to look elsewhere to broaden your view.

Sample Sites

Virtual papers

Some of the world's greatest newspapers are very generous with the amount of information they put online. You may well have to register, but all these sites will give you free information. Some may charge to search archives.

UK
- *Financial Times* – www.ft.com
- *Guardian/Observer* – www.guardian.co.uk
- *Independent* – www.independent.co.uk
- *Sunday Times* – www.sunday-times.co.uk
- *Daily Telegraph* – www.telegraph.co.uk
- *The Times* – www.thetimes.co.uk

US
- *Boston Globe* – www.bostonglobe.com
- *New York Times* – www.nytimes.com
- *USA Today* – www.usatoday.com
- *Washington Post* – www.washingtonpost.com

Global
- Newspaper library – www.ipl.org/reading/news
- *Irish Times* – www.ireland.com
- *Le Monde* – www.lemonde.fr
- *Die Welt* – www.welt.de

The Web isn't restricted to big names – many local newspapers have their own sites too. The address will generally be mentioned in the paper and at their offices. If you don't get your local rag, but would like to see what it's up to – or you want to revisit the local news from your birthplace, try looking up the newspaper in a search engine.

Broadcasters online

Because the Web is a strange mixture of print and broadcasting, it's not surprising that the TV companies have got into online news in just as big a way as the newspapers. In fact, because of their need to stay up to the minute, the TV companies' news sites are usually updated more frequently than the papers, though they may have less commentary.

The trouble with news sites, comprehensive though they may be, is the need to go and look at them. If it all seems too much trouble, there is an alternative. A number of news sites provide a service where a bulletin is mailed to you weekly, daily or even more frequently. With the better sites, you can even tailor the sort of news you want in your bulletin, building your own online newspaper.

Provided your e-mail package can handle HTML (the format used by the World Wide Web) these bulletins can be neatly laid out, and include headlines which you can click to get extra information. Unless you are permanently connected to the Web, clicking such a link will dial up again to get the extra information.

One step ahead of the e-mailed bulletin is the desktop headline service. Some news providers supply little programs that sit on your computer desktop displaying headlines. If you want to know more about the story, you can click on the headline and get the latest information. These programs are quite separate from your Web browser, but will need to dial up to get the latest information if you aren't permanently connected to the Web. Headline services come in two flavours. Some are standalone programs; others are 'active components' for the Windows desktop, sitting as part of your backdrop. In either case, you set the interval at which you want the headlines to be updated, and the program pulls down information accordingly.

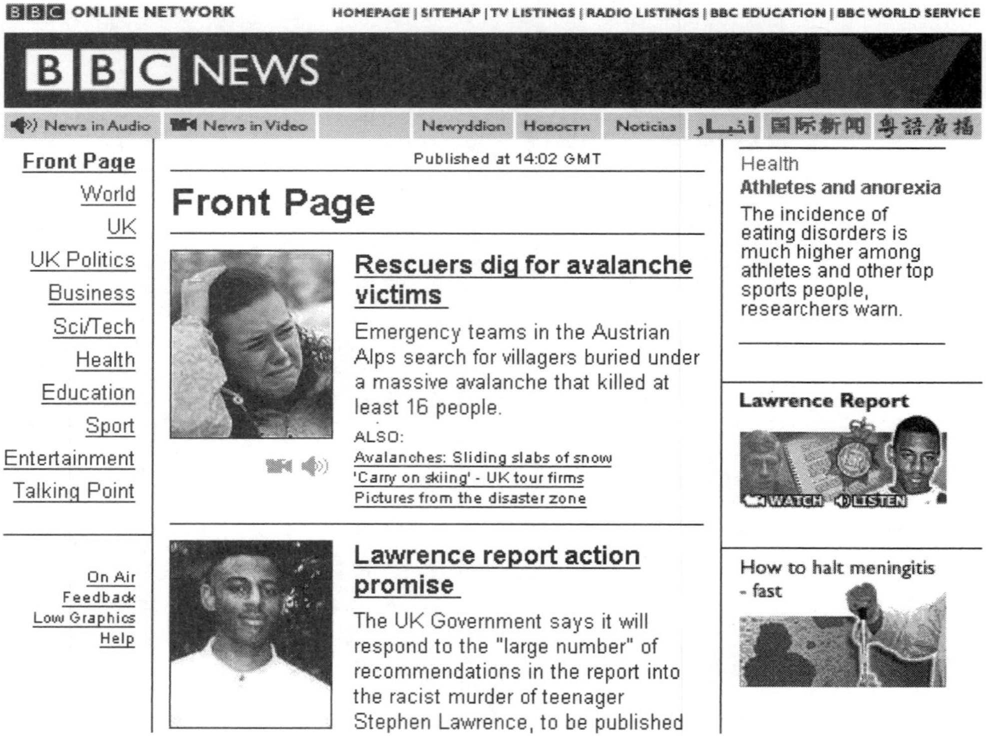

BBC ONLINE NETWORK
HOMEPAGE | SITEMAP | TV LISTINGS | RADIO LISTINGS | BBC EDUCATION | BBC WORLD SERVICE
BBC NEWS
News in Audio
News in Video
Newyddion
Новости
Noticias
أخبار
国际新闻
粤語廣播
Front Page
World
UK
UK Politics
Business
Sci/Tech
Health
Education
Sport
Entertainment
Talking Point
On Air
Feedback
Low Graphics
Help
Published at 14:02 GMT
Front Page
Rescuers dig for avalanche victims
Emergency teams in the Austrian Alps search for villagers buried under a massive avalanche that killed at least 16 people.
ALSO:
Avalanches: Sliding slabs of snow
'Carry on skiing' - UK tour firms
Pictures from the disaster zone
Lawrence report action promise
The UK Government says it will respond to the "large number" of recommendations in the report into the racist murder of teenager Stephen Lawrence, to be published
Health
Athletes and anorexia
The incidence of eating disorders is much higher among athletes and other top sports people, researchers warn.
Lawrence Report
WATCH
LISTEN
How to halt meningitis - fast

Figure 7.2 TV news on a Web site (BBC)

(**Sample Sites**)

TV news sites

It's well worth looking at sites both inside your country and outside to get a wider perspective on the news.

UK
- BBC – if you're only going for one news site, it ought to be this – news.bbc.co.uk
- News Now (pulls news from other sources) – www.newsnow. co.uk
- Sky News – www.skynews.co.uk
- Teletext – www.teletext.co.uk

US
- ABC – www.abcnews.com
- CBS – www.cbs.com
- CNN – www.cnn.com
- NBC/ Microsoft – www.nbc.com

World
- CBC – Canadian Broadcasting Corporation – www.newsworld. cbc.ca

---

Agencies

Real news junkies can go one stage further and get news from the horse's mouth. While huge news operations like the BBC and ITN manage to have correspondents all over the globe, many papers and TV companies are dependent on news agencies, which provide 'pure' news without any editorial contribution. Also known as wire services from their historical means of distribution, probably the best known agencies are Reuters and Associated Press. While agencies might not give the same depth as the papers and TV, they are sometimes the first with a story.

The good news is that most news agencies have their own sites and freely pump out information that their clients have to pay for (admittedly, they get it sooner, but you can hardly complain). If you want your news 'pure' and early, try an agency.

Increasingly there are also Web-based news services that don't have an allegiance to a particular newspaper, TV channel or terrestrial agencies. From the green-haired virtual presenter of Ananova to the general news search facilities like Moreover, these services can provide the news tailored to your personal requirements.

Sample Sites

News agencies

Many news agencies have worldwide coverage, but as always the flavours differ considerably.

UK
- Ananova – www.ananova.com – complete with virtual newscaster
- Press Association – www.pa.press.net
- Reuters – www.reuters.com

US
- Associated Press – wire.ap.org
- United Press International – www.upi.com

SEARCH
- Excite – nt.excite.com
- Moreover – www.moreover.com
- News Index – www.newsindex.com

Global
- Agence France Presse – www.afp.com
- Kyodo (Japan) – home.kyodo.co.jp
- TASS (Russia) – itar-tass.com
- Xinhua (China) – www.xinhua.org

TV and radio listings

There's a hybrid set of information that falls somewhere between broadcast news and a magazine – TV and radio schedules. With digital services bringing hundreds of new channels online there has never been more need for a comprehensive listings service. These online services often allow the user to develop a personal profile of the channels they are interested in, rather than wading through pages of irrelevant listings. Try the site of your favourite listings magazine, or use an index to dig out the best places for listings.

WEATHER OR NOT...

Although all the online news services provide some form of weather information, it can be quite summary, or irrelevant to your part of the world. Luckily, the weather enthusiast can also find specific weather sites that are dedicated to everything you could possibly want to know about the subject. From the latest satellite maps to detailed forecasts for your part of the country, these weather services will provide hours of entertainment for fans of the shipping forecast. Try an index for a good list of sites.

Sample Sites

TV and radio listings

UK
- *Radio Times* – www.radiotimes.beeb.com
- Scene One – www.sceneone.co.uk

US
- Ultimate TV – www.ultimatetv.com
- Yahoo – tv.yahoo.com

Sample Sites

Weather

Weather services give most information about their own area, but most of them also provide worldwide data.

UK
- BBC (again) www.bbc.co.uk/weather
- Met Office – www.metoffice.com
- Online Weather – www.onlineweather.com
- Satellite images – http://www.nottingham.ac.uk/meteosat

US
- Accuweather – www.accuweather.com
- Intellicast – www.intellicast.com
- Weather Channel – www.weather.com

STOCKS AND SHARES

A specialist form of news interest is how your personal stocks and shares are doing. Many news services carry share price highlights, but there are free services which will monitor your personal portfolio, letting you know just how you are doing. At their most basic, these will give you recent prices on a list of shares, but some will even allow you to enter the details of your holdings, then keep you up-to-date with your overall gains and losses.

Such services generally rely on the stock exchange code for the shares you are interested in. Usually there will be a method of looking these up first. Bear in mind also that many services are US-oriented and may only provide listings of the US exchange – but hunting around should provide you with the right information.

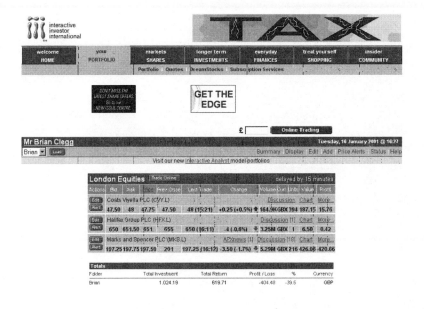

Figure 7.3 Online investment portfolio (Interactive Investor)

Sample Sites

Stocks and shares

Share sites and tickers that keep you up-to-date with your personal share portfolio. You can often also get share prices from news sites and portal sites.

UK
- Find – www.find.co.uk
- Interactive Investor – www.iii.co.uk
- Money Extra – www.moneyextra.co.uk

US
- Money Central – moneycentral.msn.com
- Quote – fast.quote.com/fq/quotecom/quote

E-MAGS

Magazines, like newspapers, put a surprising amount of their content online, though you may have to subscribe to get access to the full content. You can always resort to a search engine or index, but you may well be able to guess a magazine's web address. As with the advice on people's names in e-mail addresses, try running the words together or with hyphens – not to mention common abbreviations. Often the site is actually arranged under the publisher's name – if you happen to know that, it's another good one to try – but individual magazines will usually have their own addresses too.

Sample Sites

Magazines

The range of magazine sites is huge – this is just a taster. Use the magazines section of an index to get a wider sample.

Computing
- *Hot Wired* –www.hotwired.com
- *VNU* (includes *Personal Computer World*) – www.vnu.co.uk
- *Ziff Davies* (includes *PC Magazine*) – www.zdnet.co.uk

News
- *Economist* – www.economist.com
- *Newsweek* – www.newsweek.com

General
- *New Scientist* – www.newscientist.com
- *Readers Digest* – www.readersdigest.com
- *Smithsonian* – www.smithsonianmag.si.edu
- *V3* (lifestyle and technology) – www.v3.co.uk

E-BOOKS

The e-book has thrown many publishers into turmoil. An e-book is a whole book, packaged up on the Web in such a way that it can be downloaded and read at ease. Formats include those designed for ordinary PCs, palmtops and specialist book readers. The concept has publishers worried as it is possible for an author to sell direct to the reader – without the publisher taking a cut. In practice, e-books have not proved much of a threat so far, as there is no way of reading them that compares with a real book for convenience and ease of use. Even so, e-books exist, and will continue to take a slice of the market.

Sample Sites

E-books

These sites offer varying formats of e-book for download, usually at a price, though some are free. Increasingly you will also find e-book versions of existing books on sale at the publisher's Web site.

- Barnes and Noble – www.barnesandnoble.com
- Booklocker – www.booklocker.com
- eBook Mall – www.ebookmall.com

FOCUS

People, places, business and education

- Getting in touch;
- Locating people;
- Where is it?
- What's there?
- What do they do?

WHO, WHERE, HOW...

The Internet, particularly the Web, is a worldwide network of people, organizations and companies – so what better way of finding them? Perhaps you want a company's telephone number or the e-mail address of an old college friend. Perhaps you need some biographical details of a person you are researching, or the address of a university on the other side of the world. As usual, the Internet won't answer every question, but it's a great place to try.

E-MAIL, PLEASE

E-mail has huge advantages over the conventional mail. It's vastly quicker, much cheaper and very flexible. It has advantages over telephoning too. There are no worries about different time zones when sending a message halfway around the world – and it doesn't even matter if the recipient isn't there right now. The telephone does have one big advantage, though – directories. You'll probably have a telephone directory in your house. It may be clumsy, but it does give a practical way of looking up a number (and often an address) of someone local. If you need to go further afield, there is always directory enquiries. So what do you do when you want someone's e-mail address?

You might be able to guess. Like Web addresses, e-mail addresses come in a standard form. Don't listen to the people who think they're being funny, moaning about e-mail addresses being impossible because they're all this dot that dot the other (dot). Next time you watch a TV show which gives out an e-mail address and a telephone number, concentrate on each briefly. Then half an hour later, try to remember them. Usually the e-mail address will be much more likely to stick in your mind, especially if you get the idea of how the address is put together. It's made up of something that tells you about the person, an 'at' sign (@) and something that tells you about the company or organization the person is involved with, or uses to get the Internet.

So, my address is brian@cul.co.uk:

- brian – my name;
- cul – my company (Creativity Unleashed Limited, and yes, I do know what cul means in French);
- co.uk – because it's a UK-based company.

The part after the @ sign is relatively easy, because it's like the end of a Web address. If you know, for example, that someone works for a particular company, you can try name@company.com or name@company.co.uk (or whatever your particular country ending is – see the Endings Zoom in on page 23). Remember to ring the changes on the company. You might like to find the company's Web site first, to see whether it uses TheBigCompany, The_Big_Company, The-Big-Company, TBC or even BigCo. Although it's not obliged to, chances are it will use the same format for Web site and e-mail address. Anyway, if you find the site, you will probably also find a few sample e-mail addresses on it to get an idea of the format.

You'll have to ring the changes a bit on the name part too. I have seen a name like mine represented in all these ways:

- Brian;
- BrianClegg;
- Brian_Clegg;
- Brian.Clegg;
- BrianC;
- BClegg;
- Brian_M_Clegg;
- Brian.M.Clegg.

(Purists point out that there shouldn't be dots to the left of the @ sign, but it doesn't stop people doing it.) Don't assume that just because a company is big it will insist on full names: famously, Bill Gates' address is billg@microsoft.com. Note that, thankfully, e-mail addresses aren't case sensitive, so Brian and brian are treated the same. It's Internet convention to use all lowercase, but if it makes it clearer, especially where names are run together, use capitals.

If you want to use the guessing technique, don't be afraid to give it a go. If the address you type in is wrong, you will get an automatic message back saying so – no one will get angry about it. Bear in mind, though that there could be other people with the same name at the company (or at another company with a similar address), so make sure that the initial message you send is short and polite.

If you use a large Internet service provider, you may be in luck. The big boys generally have an internal directory service where you can search for a Floyd Goosegrease who lives in Florida (or whatever), but success with this depends on the person you want to contact using the same ISP. Out in the big wide world of the Internet, it's a much darker and uncertain place. You may not be able to get an e-mail address at all. If you can, you may need a degree of stealth. However, before getting clever, let's be straight-forward. There may not be phone books, but there are directories. A number of companies offer searchable lists of e-mail addresses.

You will find such listings on standalone sites, (some include tele-phone and address too) and on most portal sites too. You can also access a number of these directly from the more sophisticated e-mail packages. For instance, in Microsoft Outlook, if you are addressing an e-mail, click on the To... button and then the Find... button, you will see a box that will link directly to half a dozen of the big name people directories.

Figure 8.1 A UK white pages (ukphonebook.com)

Sample Sites

White pages

Global e-mail, telephone and address:

- Infospace – www.infospace.com
- Peoplesearch – www.peoplesearch.com – white pages metasearch
- Any Who – www.anywho.com

Global e-mail, US telephone and address:

- Bigfoot – www.bigfoot.com
- Four 11 – www.four11.com
- Any Who – www.anywho.com
- Switchboard – www.switchboard.com
- Who Where – www.whowhere.lycos.com

UK telephone and address:

- 192 – www.192.com – includes electoral roll data. Some charged
- BT Directory Enquiries – www.phonenetuk.bt.com
- Royal Mail postcode/address finder – www.royalmail.co.uk/paf
- UK Phonebook – www.ukphonebook.com

UK e-mail

- Yahoo – people.yahoo.co.uk

There is also a meta e-mail address search engine:

- MESA – mesa.rrzn.uni-hannover.de

It's not all plain sailing using White Pages. Most people's e-mail addresses change over time. White Page directory sites only get hold of an e-mail address where they're told it (why not add yours while you are there?) or come across it somewhere, so not infrequently you will either get multiple addresses or an old one. If you are given multiple addresses, it shouldn't do any harm to try them all (within reason!). If an address no longer exists, the message will simply be returned to you unsent.

If you don't get anywhere with the directories, where next? Try a search on the person's name. See Chapter 4 if you need a reminder about using search engines. It's worth using a few different search engines. Use the name in its most common form (see the Zoom in What name?) as a phrase. Try the individual words, or variants on the name. It may seem unlikely that one individual would come up out of the whole world, but it's surprising how often you can succeed. Putting my own name into AltaVista came up with about 120 references. I found six or seven 'Brian Clegg's, of which I was one. If the person you are searching for happens to be called Gillian Anderson (or a similarly famous name) you will be flooded with results. In such circumstances, it's worth trying something like "gillian anderson" and not (xfiles or x-files).

What name?

Of course you know the name of the person you are looking for – but remember that computers are less flexible than humans when it comes to searching. If you were on the lookout for David Merricks, you could scan a list and pick out D. Merricks, Mr D M Merricks, Dave Merricks or even the subtle variation David Merrick without problem. Computers are rarely that clever.

Start with the most common public form of someone's name. Just because you call the person Twinky, it doesn't mean the name will appear like that in print. If the person generally uses a shorter version of his or her name, try both that and the full name. If there's a middle initial, but it's rarely used, try without it first, then with. For hyphenated names, be prepared to try with a hyphen, a space or no gap at all.

Trying these variants on a person's name may not deliver the goods, but you are much more likely to be effective.

Finding someone in a search engine doesn't guarantee you'll get the e-mail address. But following up the more obvious links, you may well find a page where the address is listed. What if this fails? You could look for the name in likely newsgroups, but you may need to go beyond the Internet. Increasingly, e-mail addresses appear in all sorts of locations. Might there be some printed publication which would carry this person's address – a magazine or book or leaflet? As we saw in Chapter 6, I found a number of e-mail addresses in *Who's Who* – if even this stately publication carries them, they could be in print anywhere.

Another possibility is to try the various groupings the person may be part of. For example, schools, colleges and universities increasingly have

zoom in

'alumni' pages, listing contact details for old students. If you know the company the person works for, and haven't got anywhere with the suggestions above for guessing an e-mail format, you could find the company's Web site and send a message to their info e-mail address or equivalent. They might not help, but they may be able to give you an address.

When you've got an address, err on the side of caution. Remember that in a worldwide community, it's pretty likely that you will have two people with the same name. Unless you are certain, don't plunge in with a very personal message – a polite enquiry first is a good move.

Try It

Your name

This is a double-value exercise. It's human nature to look yourself up in the index of a book that covers something you've been involved in – similarly it's hard to resist seeing if there's something about you in the online world.

Start with the directories. See how you are listed (if at all) in some of the big name online directories (see the Sample sites White Pages above). If you aren't listed, or the listings are wrong, consider correcting them. After all, it might help someone else find you.

Now move on to the search engines. Don't worry if you don't find anything – the Web is anything but comprehensive. But if your name does occur, spend a few minutes browsing the search results. Do this even if it's obvious that the person referred to isn't you – the results can be fascinating. By doing this, in one search engine alone I've found myself and all these other 'Brian Clegg's:

- a clay pigeon shooter;
- a hockey player;
- an art materials manufacturer;
- a PCB designer;
- an elderly man in the news for bringing home a young bride from Thailand;
- a managing director of an electronics firm;
- a basketball coach;
- a printer;
- a businessman in my home town;
- a man charged with larceny by the US grand jury;
- plus a history of my surname.

ADDRESS AND PHONE

Finding an address or phone number takes a step away from the business of the Internet itself – out of the virtual world into the physical world. It doesn't make it impractical to use the Internet as a source, though. Most of the White Pages (see Sample sites on page 100) offer telephone and address searches for the US. Similar facilities exist for the UK (see above), though limitations on the data mean that achieving a result is sometimes a little more complex – even so, with perseverance you will usually get there.

An alternative approach if you know where the person you wish to contact works is to get in touch this way. We've already seen the use of the company site to get hold of an e-mail address. It will usually also provide a correspondence address and a telephone switchboard number, which should put you well on the way to getting in touch.

WHAT ARE THEY DOING?
WHO ARE THEY ANYWAY?

Sometimes our interest in people isn't in communicating with them, but rather finding out more about them. They might be a composer whose music you find interesting, an old college friend you want to keep track of, or a business rival you need to check out. This is a quest that repays quite lengthy work with search engines. Try the different name formats in different engines. Be prepared to work through quite a few of the results, just in case it's the right person.

If the person you are researching is at all in the public eye, you will start to build up a picture of that person. If the person is academic, you can get a feel for the papers he or she has presented or books he or she has written (try looking the person up in the online bookshops). Perhaps there are conferences or seminars the person has been involved in. If the person is involved in the arts or sport, you can look out for reviews or commentary. Perhaps the person has hobbies that will get him or her mentioned, or a personal Web site. One place specifically worth investigating if you are looking for details of a famous person is the imaginatively titled www.biography.com – which contains just what you might expect.

CLIMBING THE FAMILY TREE

There's a very specific aspect of people that the Internet can help with – genealogy. Whether you are trying to reconstruct your family tree in splendid detail or simply want to know a bit more about your name and where it comes from, there's a good chance you can get help from the Internet.

There are two directions you can start in here – one is in getting tools and tips on the business of researching your family tree; the other is in finding information about your name and your specific branch of that family. The sample sites below give some pointers on getting started, and contacts with others who are interested in genealogy. To find out more about your own surname, and what others have already found out, try something like yourname and (genealogy or research) in a search engine. Take a look also at genforum.com, which hosts a mass of forums to discuss different surnames and ask for information.

Sample Sites

Genealogy

Some general sites on genealogy:

- Cyndi's List – www.cyndislist.com
- Family Search – www.familysearch.org – massive Mormon database
- National Genealogy Society – www.ngsgenealogy.org
- Online Genealogical Database – www.gentree.com
- Treasure Maps – www.firstct.com/fv/tmapmenu.html
- UK & Ireland Genealogy Index – www.genuki.org.uk

FINDING PLACES

The first point of call for simply locating a town, business or educational establishment is liable to be a specific Web site. Most companies and colleges have them, and increasingly towns and cities do too (especially those with tourist value). Try the obvious site names (see page 22 for hints). It's also worth trying a search engine even if you have found the site, as you may find an unofficial page with more information. Generally this is enough to get hold of an address or other location details. *Yellow Pages* style directories can also help with addresses: see page 110.

Hopefully you've now got an address, which is fine, but you can't beat a good map when it comes to finding your way around. If the location information you have found doesn't have a map (often a Web site will include one), the Internet is increasingly a good source of maps, sometimes going down to a startling level of detail. Inevitably, the best mapping is available for the US, but increasingly maps are being added for other parts of the world too.

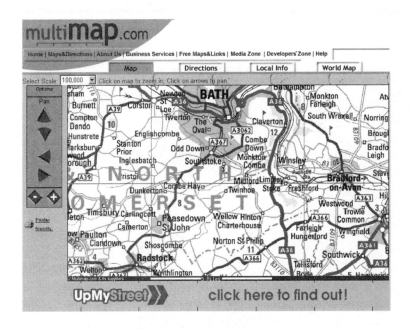

Figure 8.2 Online mapping in the UK (Multimap)

Sample Sites

Maps

Try these sites for getting online maps and route information:

US and Europe
- Expedia – www.expediamaps.com
- Maps Index – www.mapsindex.com
- Terraserver – www.terraserver.com

UK
- GetMapping (aerial photographs) – www.getmapping.com
- Multimap – uk.multimap.com

UK
- World maps – www.lib.utexas.edu/Libs/PCL/Map_collection/Map_collection.html

---

GETTING THERE

Once your location is established, you need to get there. If you are driving you will need route directions. If you'd like someone else to do the driving (or flying), the Web can come in handy for checking timetables and even making reservations. If you intend to travel outside your own country, the worldwide facilities can be great – but if you intend to make a booking this way, check out the comments on security on page 28.

Sample Sites

Getting there

Most travel companies now have Web sites, many providing timetables and even booking facilities. Here is a sample:

Driving Routes
- AA – www.theaa.com – UK
- Maporama – www.maporama.com – Europe
- Map Blast – www.mapblast.com – US

- Map Quest – www.mapquest.com – US
- RAC – www.rac.co.uk – UK

Airlines

- Air France – www.airfrance.co.uk
- American – www.aa.com
- British Airways – www.british-airways.com
- Lufthansa – www.lufthansa.de
- United – www.ual.com
- US Air – www.usair.com
- Virgin – www.virginatlantic.com

Railways

- European timetable – www.eurorail.com/railsked.htm
- Railtrack (UK timetable) – www.railtrack.co.uk
- SNCF (French Railways) – www.sncf.fr/indexe.htm
- Swiss Railways – www.sbb.ch/index_e.htm
- The Trainline (UK rail bookings) – www.thetrainline.com

WHAT'S THERE?

So you know where you are going and how to get there, but what facilities are there in the town? What are the sightseeing possibilities in your planned holiday destination? Can you find a decent restaurant? While the first port of call will be to check out Web sites that cover the town or region you are visiting, you could try a totally different direction. For example, if you are looking for a pub, you could look under the place, but you might equally check out a pub guide. Similarly, looking for sporting facilities you might get more information from a sporting site. There are a few sites listed below; otherwise try appropriate keywords in a search engine, or (even better) look under the travel section of an index.

This is a particularly appropriate subject for getting help from people. Do you know someone who lives nearby who can give you some tips? Is there a newsgroup or forum where you can ask for recommendations? Often a personal recommendation will be a lot more valuable than a bland Web site. However good a hotel guide might be, you can't beat contacting someone who has just stayed there. They are much more likely to tell you the little personal details that make so much difference.

Sample Sites

What's there

Some general sites for locating facilities and features:

UK
- AA Guides (UK) – www.theaa.co.uk
- British Tourist Authority – www.visitbritain.com
- Expedia – www.expedia.co.uk
- London Town – www.londontown.com
- Pub World (UK) – www.pubworld.co.uk
- Sightseeing – www.sightseeing.co.uk
- UK Resort Guide – www.resort-guide.co.uk

US/World
- City Search – national.citysearch.com
- Excite Travel – www.city.net
- Go United States – www.go-unitedstates.com
- USA City Link – usacitylink.com

WHAT'S ON?

You might just want to go to the local cinema, or be about to visit a remote city for a weekend break and would like to know what's on. Perhaps you want to get tickets for the latest Lloyd Webber, or find out if your favourite comedian has a tour in your vicinity this year. The Web is a particularly effective place to find answers to this sort of question, because many entertainment companies have realized the potential the Web has as a vehicle for marketing.

For a trip to the movies, you will be able to find a 'what's on' site that lists every film showing at your local multiplex, down to times, a review of the films and contact numbers – everything you need to make a decision. With other forms of entertainment you may need to search a little more. Do you know the theatre or sports ground involved? If so, you can check if the venue has its own Web site. Alternatively, try searching for the performer's name, the name of the show or the name of the team. One of these approaches will generally yield the information you are looking for.

(**Sample Sites**)

What's on

Theatre and cinema listings, and more:

UK
- London listings – www.thisislondon.com
- TheatreNet – www.theatrenet.co.uk
- TheatreWeb – www.uktw.co.uk
- Virgin – what's on at UK cinemas – www.virgin.net/cinema/filmfinder
- What's On Stage – www.whatsonstage.com

US
- City Search – national.citysearch.com
- Hollywood.com – showtimes.hollywood.com
- Playbill – www.playbill.com
- Yahoo – movies.yahoo.com

BUSINESSES

Many businesses now have their own Web sites, on which they will usually provide contact information. With many companies you can guess the Web site (see page 22 for some hints on guessing addresses). Failing that, use the search engine techniques from Chapter 4 to find the company on the Web.

In some cases, though, the company simply won't have a Web site, or perhaps you don't want a specific business, but rather a leather goods shop in the Brighton area. In that case, you are better off turning to a subject directory (Yellow Pages). You will find them significantly more flexible than the paper version. For example, in the UK Yellow Pages, you can start a search in a particular place, but then widen it to include a bigger area until you are covering the whole of the country.

Like the real *Yellow Pages*, it can sometimes take a couple of tries to hit the right name for what you are looking for (famously, for several years the UK *Yellow Pages* carried an entry 'Boring – see Civil Engineers'), but should the directory be fussy, there is usually a way of checking through a list of categories.

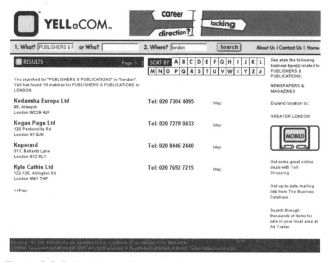

Figure 8.3 Online Yellow Pages result (Yell)

Sample Sites

Subject directories

Subject directories are the Yellow Pages of the Web – in fact, not surprisingly, some of the best known are actually the electronic version of *Yellow Pages* itself.

UK

- Scoot – www.scoot.co.uk
- Thomson – www.thomweb.co.uk
- Yellow Pages – www.yell.co.uk

US
- Superpages – www.superpages.com
- Yellow Pages – www.yellowpages.com

Global
- World Pages – www.worldpages.com

For those interested in businesses, there is a category of information resources that specializes in everything you want to know about a particular business. You can discover company profiles, financial performance data, competitive information and more. Not surprisingly, much of this information costs. Business intelligence is an expensive game. Even so, getting this information on the Web is one of the cheapest and certainly the most convenient way of getting hold of it.

Sample Sites

Business intelligence

Many of these sites are US-based but will cover major UK companies:

- Bird Online – www.bird-online.co.uk
- Daily Stocks – www.dailystocks.com
- Dun & Bradstreet – www.dnb.com
- Equifax – www.equifax.co.uk
- Hoovers – www.hoovers.com
- The Motley Fool – www.fool.co.uk and www.fool.com
- *Wall Street Journal* – www.wsj.com

EDUCATION

Colleges, schools and universities are all very aware of the benefits of having a presence on the Web. Whether you want to check out the courses – sometimes including as much detail as reading lists and synopses of lectures – or just to have a look at the location, you will find many educational centres listed. You'll normally find it easy enough to find these sites via a search engine or index (guessing isn't always easy as abbreviations are often used), but some of the better-known sites, and some sites listing universities are provided below. While ac and edu (US) are the most common endings for educational addresses, sch for school has started to appear as well.

Sample Sites

Colleges and universities

Practically every university has a Web site. Here are a few of the better-known establishments, plus some links sites that list appropriate addresses.

UK
- Cambridge – www.cam.ac.uk
- Durham – www.durham.ac.uk
- Open University – www.open.ac.uk
- Oxford – www.ox.ac.uk

US
- Harvard – www.harvard.edu
- MIT – web.mit.edu
- Yale – www.yale.edu

Links sites
- American universities – www.clas.ufl.edu/CLAS/american-universities.html
- Peterson's (US) Directory – www.petersons.com
- UK Universities – www.dfee.gov.uk/info/univer.htm
- Worldwide Universities – www.findaschool.org

---

9 FOCUS
Expertise and archives

- Using free expertise;
- Following links and rings;
- Magazines and archives;
- Getting hold of images, sounds and pictures.

AMONGST THE EXPERTS AND ARCHIVISTS

A lot of Web use involves general research. Don't be put off by the R word – we aren't necessarily talking about in-depth academic work here (though that wouldn't be unusual). Instead, you could be getting background material for an article, helping with some homework or just following up a personal interest. Whatever the topic, the chances are that there is an expert out there with a Web site or chatting in a newsgroup. It's only a matter of finding the right place.

If you need material like photographs, sound or video, the Web is also the place to go. It's not all about words. In fact, it's arguable that without the impact of multimedia it would never have got as popular as it has. There are millions of pictures up there of all sorts of subjects. There are sounds too, from plinky-plonky MIDI files for picking out a tune on a sound card, to full CD-quality audio. There's even video from the ropy to the robust. If you are looking for media to support your research, to use as part of a presentation or simply to brighten up your PC's backdrop, the Web is a good place to look.

LINKING ON

Web-based experts tend not only to provide lots of information for free, but to point you towards other helpful sources. It's here that the technique of linking on comes into its own. If you are using software like a ferret to support your search (see Chapter 5), you may simply have to press a button to follow up the links. Otherwise, it's certainly worth spending a few minutes skimming around the links, finding which seem the most likely sites. After all, the first site you reach may not be the most appropriate for what you want. Remember to book-mark the sites which are particularly promising so you don't get too lost in a process which can often involve following links from links (… and so on).

RINGING THE CHANGES

A particularly valuable resource if you want an in-depth look at a subject is a Web ring. This sounds more dramatic (even Wagnerian) than it really is. A Web ring is simply a number of sites about a particular sub-ject whose owners have agreed to provide links that travel from site to site in a ring. The ring allows you to jump on to the next site when you have finished with the current one, gradually building a better picture of the topic. You will often come across a Web ring entry in the form of a banner at the top or bottom of a site, which will then lead you on to other sites. Some of these are quite sophisticated, giving you options to jump around the ring at random or list the next ten sites.

Web rings aren't a substitute for using a search engine, as they depend on someone else's idea of what fits a certain category, and the site you really need might take a long time to hit on a large ring. Even so, if your prime motive is exploring a topic rather than homing in on a specific site, a Web ring can prove very valuable.

(**Sample Sites**)

Web rings

If you haven't found a ring when exploring your topic, you could try the Web ring directories:

- RingSurf – www.ringsurf.com
- Yahoo! (formerly Web Ring) – www.webring.com

or alternatively you might like to try an index (most likely under computing/internet heading) or a search engine by combining your topic with webring or web ring.

MAGAZINES ON THE WEB

We've already seen in the reference section (page 94) how magazines have a significant presence on the Web. As well as offering general reading matter, magazines often provide a good source of expertise. After all, many specialist magazines have expert authors writing for them. If you pick a title that is dedicated to the topic you are researching, they should be a good background source. More Web-conscious magazines may even have live links to other appropriate sites.

If you know of a publication, you can hunt for its Web site and use the search feature you will invariably find on the magazine's site to dig out appropriate topics. If not, use an index or the refining technique of checking a general search engine's responses for sites that appear to be magazines covering the subject. Then go to the magazine's site, find the search page and look internally in depth.

DIGITAL ARCHIVES

If you are very lucky, your special topic might be featured in a digital archive (often called digital libraries). These are almost digital museums, providing an exploration of a particular subject through photographs, documents and other archive material. This is quite a different prospect to the online books described on page 17. This is not material from a single source, but a compendium of pictures and text. As with many Web resources, there's a strong US bias in the information available, but more and more academic institutions are providing material online, expanding this type of resource.

Sample Sites

Digital archives

You may well hit digital archives when using a search engine. Here are a few of the better-known sites:

- American Memory Project – lcweb2.loc.gov/ammem
- British Library – www.bl.uk
- UK National Museum of Science and Industry – www.nmsi.ac.uk
- US National Archives – www.nara.gov
- University of California Digital Library – sunsite.berkeley.edu
- World Art Treasures – sgwww.epfl.ch/berger

FINDING PICTURES, SOUNDS AND VIDEO

Because most Web sites are multimedia you will find media elements like pictures, sound and video scattered all over the Web. Using a general search engine is not a bad starting point, especially if you include a keyword like picture, photograph, photo, sound, music or video. There are, however, specialist sites and search engines which concentrate on photographs and other media. These sites may be dedicated to a single topic (often a popular TV or movie star), or may be the home of a visual collection, just as a museum may house a collection of physical photographs. One big advantage of some of the specialist search engines is that they return thumbnails – tiny copies of the picture – so you can get an idea of what it is like without following up each result.

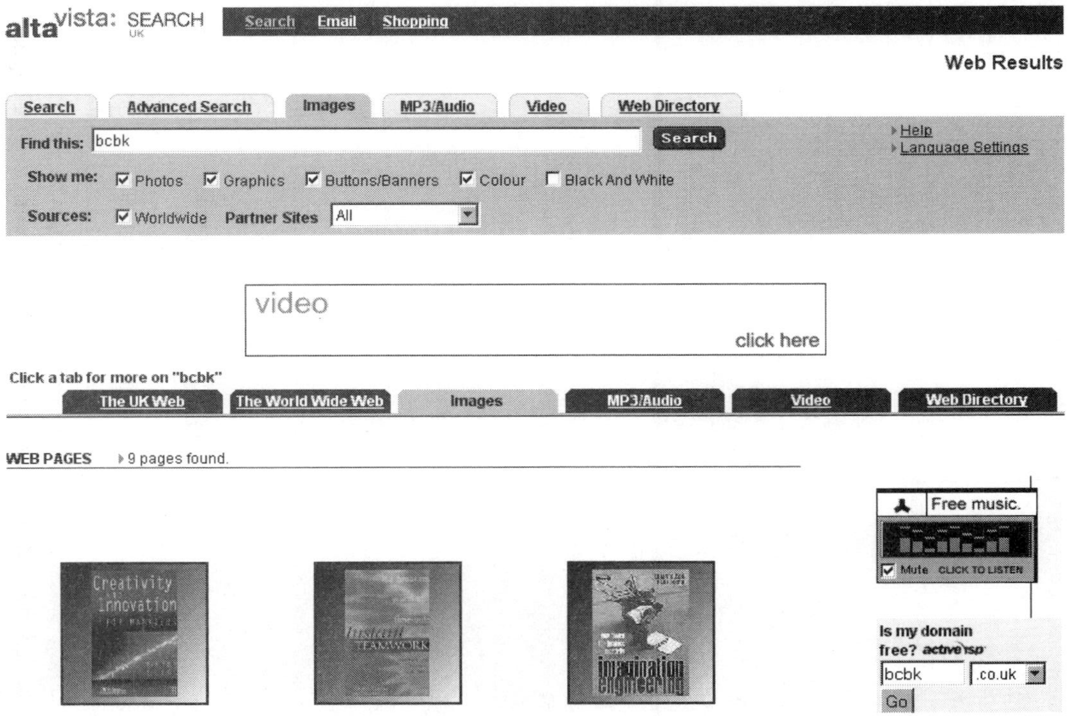

Figure 9.1 Image search engine results (AltaVista)

Some specialist search engines also have built-in filters to try to minimize the chances of accidentally turning up a pornographic image. These can never be entirely accurate. If you don't object to possibly offensive thumbnail images, it may be worth switching the filter off as it is entirely possible for legitimate images to be accidentally removed as well.

It is also worth checking out the relevant newsgroups. You will often find newsgroups with keywords like photos, pictures, binary and binaries, which specialize in attachments of this kind.

Sample Sites

Pictures, sounds and video

Many of the specialist search engines return thumbnails of photos. Some, like Scour, cover all the media, others are more limited.

- All Music Guide – allmusic.com
- Arriba Vista – www.arribavista.com
- AltaVista Multimedia Search – www.altavista.com
- Lycos – multimedia.lycos.com
- MP3.com – www.mp3.com
- Music Search – www.musicsearch.com
- Pictures Now – www.picturesnow.com
- The Silvis Woodshed (MIDI choral files) – www.channel1.com/users/gsilvis
- Scour – scour.net

GRABBING A PICTURE

Pictures are easy to handle with Web browsers. Once you are viewing the picture on the screen, right click it with your mouse (Mac users will have a key/mouse combination). You will be given the option of saving it to disk or (probably) of making it the backdrop on your PC.

Assuming you do save the file, you then need to do something with it. Photographs on the Web are mostly in one of four formats. New ones emerge every couple of years, but these will remain the common ones for some time. Most popular is JPEG (sometimes called JPG, which is the file extension used on PCs), a 'lossy' compressed format. Lossy means that in the process of compressing the picture (making it take up less space on your disk than it should need), some amount of detail is sacrificed. JPEG pictures are 'true colour' with a full range of up to 16 million different colours, but of variable quality depending on how much compression is used.

An alternative format is GIF. GIFs are still compressed, but don't lose any detail. This may seem to make them more attractive, but a GIF can only have 256 colours, and is not capable of anywhere near as much compression as JPEG. For this reason, GIF is often used for small pictures, like on-screen buttons, while JPEG is usually the standard for larger photographic illustrations.

Because of various legal complications with GIF, an alternative, PNG has been developed, but to date it is very little used. The final format you will see some of is BMP, the Windows standard format. This is not compressed and isn't usable on every type of computer, but you will still see these files sometimes.

Whichever of these formats of picture you decide to download, most modern software from word processors to presentation graphics should be able to handle them. If you have any problems, it may be necessary to use a shareware graphics program like the excellent Paintshop Pro to convert them to a different format, but this is increasingly uncommon.

HANDLING SOUNDS

Sounds come in a number of formats on the Web. Most PCs will have software to play the more standard formats, while more obscure files and other computers will generally be able to download a free or shareware player. Popular audio formats are also supported by the browsers directly, either as a background sound or appearing as a small control panel on the screen. The most common formats are detailed in the Zoom in box below.

There are two distinct types of audio. Traditionally, producing a sound has involved downloading a file to the PC, then playing it. However, this isn't a suitable approach if you want to put (say) an interview or a radio station on the Web. Here 'streaming' – where small chunks of the sound are sent down and can be played as soon as they are received – is employed. This way, the impression of a continuous broadcast can be given, though often there are glitches and hesitations.

Sound formats

These are the most common sound file formats on the Internet, though you will find others:

- AU – Once-popular audio format, now relatively uncommon, but supported by most browsers.
- MIDI – A very compact music-only sound format, which contains instructions to a synthesizer on how to play the music. How good the result is depends on the quality of the synthesizer in the sound card on your PC – often the outcome is decidedly basic.
- MP3 – Highly compressed but high quality sound using MPEG (see page 121) technology. The standard for music on the Internet. Can be played on special standalone devices as well as PCs.
- Real Audio – The definitive streaming audio format, with a big hold on the market. You may need to download a (free) player – usually there's a direct link from the site with the sound files, otherwise try www.real.com
- WAV – The standard Windows format for sampled audio (ie 'recorded' sound as opposed to MIDI). Comes in a wide range of formats from full CD stereo down to low-quality mono. Before MP3 was the widest-used non-streaming audio format, so widely supported even outside the DOS/Windows world.
- WMA – Windows Media Audio. Microsoft equivalent of MP3, claimed to have better quality at the same compression.

HANDLING VIDEO

Just like audio, there are a few standard video formats handled directly by the browsers or downloaded as files to the computer where they can then be replayed by software. Again, video divides into conventional files and streaming video, which attempts to play as you go. As video involves considerably more information than sound, video files tend to be much bigger. Unless you have a high speed link to the Internet, streaming video will tend to be small and quite jerky. But as cable modems, ADSL and other high speed links come into wider use it will become a more practical medium.

Video formats

zoom in

These are the most common video file formats on the Internet, though you will find others.

- AVI – The standard video format in Windows, hence widely used. Files are large and slow to download. Internet Explorer can handle embedded AVI (ie appearing as part of a Web page).
- MPEG – Highly compressed video, now in its second release for digital TV etc. Most modern PCs will have software to handle it.
- Real Video – Like audio, the Real company dominates streaming video. Luckily, the RealPlayer software handles both. There is usually a link to download the software from the site with the video – otherwise, try www.real.com
- QuickTime – Apple's standard video format, technically superior to AVI and widely supported on PCs as well as Apple computers.

REMEMBER COPYRIGHT

There's something about the free and easy nature of the Web that makes it tempting to forget legal matters. Generally speaking, just because something is put up on the Web (and this applies to text as well as pictures, sound and video), it doesn't mean that it is freely copyable. You should be able to look at it without a problem, but doing anything more may infringe copyright laws.

That 'may' is an absolute minefield, which is going to make a lot of lawyers happy bunnies for many years. After all, if someone in China, connecting to the Web through a Russian-owned ISP, downloads a picture from my UK-owned Web site, which is hosted on US servers owned by another UK company, whose copyright laws come into play? Often it isn't a problem. It is highly unlikely anyone is going to complain about downloading anything you find on the Web to your PC for private use. But electronic documents and pictures are too easy to copy and distribute.

Where do we draw the line? When I use a copy in my homework? When I send a copy to a few friends by e-mail? When I put a copy on the company intranet? When I put a copy on my Web site? When I include it an in-house publication? When I put copies on sale? Copyright is going to be infringed – it's up to you to remember this and at the very least put in appropriate acknowledgements. For any commercial use, you need to get permission from the owner. Having said this, you are (probably) allowed to copy a certain amount of text in the UK for specific reasons without permission – see the Fair dealing Zoom in – but bear in mind that this agreement has no legal standing.

Fair dealing

There is an agreement in the UK between the Society of Authors and the Publishers Association that allows short extracts to be quoted for special reasons without the author's permission. Note, however, that this is not part of copyright law, and was drawn up long before the Web became a factor.

Under this so-called fair dealing agreement, you can take up to 400 words from a book (or 800 words if no individual section exceeds 300), less than one third of an article or less than one quarter of a poem, but only for the purposes of quotation or reviewing, with clear acknowledgement of the author and original source. This excludes song lyrics, music, material to be used in anthologies and items where the original is so short that the whole is quoted.

However you approach copyright, bear in mind that what you are dealing with is the result of someone else's effort. If that person happened to be a woodcarver, you probably wouldn't think it was legitimate to walk into his shop, pick up a carving you liked the look of, and walk off with it without paying. For a writer, the particular set of words you see, whether it's in a book like this or a document on the Internet, is their produce which may have taken years of painstaking work. Treat it with the same respect you would a physical object.

10 FOCUS
Buy, buy, buy

- Internet shopping is a reality;
- Specialist items and commodities;
- Recommendations;
- Comparisons;
- Software online.

BUYING ON THE WEB

The World Wide Web is also a worldwide market. Increasingly you will find shops of all different types trading on the Web. Because of the special nature of Internet shopping, it provides a particularly 'research-oriented' approach. The Web isn't a great way to browse aimlessly. It doesn't have the same potential for social enjoyment as buying from real shops, with real coffee bars and entertainment. However, there are some very good reasons for shopping on the Web.

It's here and now

The most obvious benefit of shopping on the Web is immediacy. It's there when you want it (computer permitting) 24 hours a day, seven days a week. And it's there in your home, without a need to venture out into uncertain weather – not a bad thing if you live in the middle of nowhere. Web shopping is convenient in a whole different way from shopping malls because of this instant availability.

Specialist interests

Despite the diversity of shops in your high street and out-of-town malls, the fact is that the big chains have generally taken over. If you have a specialist interest, it might once have been served by a little local shop in your town. More recently you would have had to travel up to a major city. Now even that possibility can't always provide the answer. I particularly enjoy Tudor and Elizabethan church music. Now that my local stores don't stock anything other than 'classical favourites', and the specialist shop in London I used to deal with has been replaced by a restaurant, I have a problem.

Or at least, I had a problem until Web shopping took off. The opportunity to reach a much wider market than a physical shop means that there are specialist Web shops with a far greater range of options than I could ever find on a shelf. If other sources can't help, I can also go directly to the manufacturers. For example, in my particular category of interest, one of the best labels is Hyperion, which will supply CDs direct if you can't get them through conventional routes. In theory, I could always have used them direct by mail order, but buying from the Web is much more immediate and practical.

Even if you still have a specialist shop you can use, the Web can sometimes expand your horizons. A Web shop can 'stock' a much wider range of goods than a real one. When online shopping first started, there was a tendency for high street retailers to set up a site with a small subset of their range – this was a big mistake. Web shopping is about easy searching through huge choice. So where a conventional bookshop might stock tens of thousands of books, a Web bookshop has millions of titles on the list. The conventional bookshop would argue that they can order all those titles too – but you get much more information by browsing on the Web, and the business of ordering can be less troublesome too.

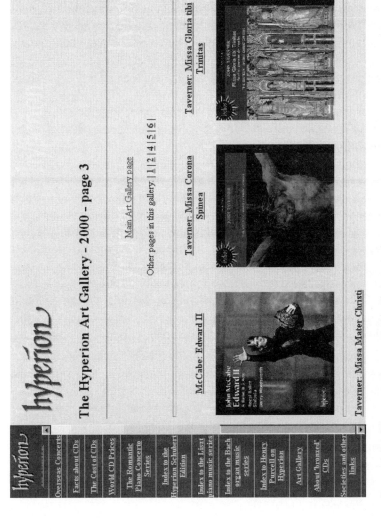

Figure 10.1 Specialist shopping online (Hyperion)

Sample Sites

Specialist shops

The range of specialist sites on the web is truly remarkable. Here are some random tasters:

- Bath robes – www.bathrobe.co.uk
- Books by Brian Clegg – www.cul.co.uk/titles
- Hyperion Records – www.hyperion-records.co.uk
- Quilting supplies – www.houseofpatchwork.co.uk
- Science Fiction shop – www.sci-fi.co.uk

Boring commodities

If special interest goods are great for Web shopping, so are the everyday items that you really don't care much about. Few people enjoy trudging around a supermarket (I have to confess that I do, but I'm unusual in this respect). Many of your supermarket purchases are the same old products – milk, bread, soup, pasta – lots of commodity items that you don't need to squeeze and enjoy browsing through. Supermarkets now allow you to place your order from the comfort of home and have the goods delivered. Some offer offline catalogues, so you can order without notching up the phone bills, and even lockable delivery boxes so your order can arrive while you are out at work. It's never going to replace all your supermarket shopping, but it does cut out the boring bits.

Advice and recommendation

We've all been in the position. You want something new and need some advice. Either you buy the latest 'What X' magazine, or you take a risk and plunge into a large shop. And a spotty assistant who has clearly only just been potty-trained can give you no help whatsoever. Sometimes you want advice, or even better, an independent recommendation.

Web shopping can help here too. A well-designed Web shop will have space to go into considerable detail about the relative merits of different products. You will also find some stores have a clever way of adding recommendation to their stock. They allow other Web sites to make recommendations on particular products based on local expertise – the products are then bought from the host site. For example, on my own site at www.cul.co.uk/books is a bookshop with recommendations in the fields of business, creativity, science fiction and popular science. Because these are areas that interest me, I can give a lot more depth and recommendation than a general purpose bookshop can. But when it comes to actually buying the book you are referred through to Amazon, the biggest Internet bookshop, which then handles all the technical areas like payment and delivery.

Something a little different

Because of the truly worldwide coverage of the Web, you can often find products from a different country that aren't readily available in your own. Small to medium-sized companies handling regional specialities from English country crafts to Florida oranges will ship you something a little different for a special treat or a present. The Web broadens your shopping horizons.

IS IT SAFE?

A frequent concern about buying over the Internet is safety. It raises the inevitable question – is it safe to use a credit card to purchase from a Web shop? As we've seen in the security section (see page 28), provided the shop uses the right security measures you are probably more safe than when giving credit card details over the phone. If you are still concerned about making a credit card order over the Internet, many Web stores provide alternatives. A typical approach would be to enter your order details via the Web, then follow it up by sending a fax or letter confirming your order and carrying your credit card details (or even a cheque or money order).

FINDING THE RIGHT PRODUCT

When you are looking for guidance on selecting a product, we've already seen how a specialist site with links to a major retailer can help.

If the product is liable to feature in a magazine's comparative review, it's worth checking out magazine sites to see how the different models match up (see page 94 for more on magazines). If you were searching for a new PC, for example, you may have two or three recommendations. It's then worth checking out the vendors' pages to see if they have any extra information. In some cases, they may even sell direct from the Web site. A sophisticated site like Dell's (www.dell.co.uk or www.dell.com) will even allow you to try out different specifications of PC and see just what you will pay for a particular requirement, without any commitment.

FINDING THE RIGHT PRICE

Be prepared to shop around. Use the search capabilities you have developed to find a number of stores offering the product you are looking for. Many Internet shops offer special discounts over and above high street shops. You can also find that an Internet shop with an international presence can provide extraordinarily good value. So, for example, the UK arm of the Amazon bookshop, Amazon.co.uk, offers many US-originated books at a lot lower than the UK list price, as long as you are prepared to wait a little longer for them to be sourced from the US. I recently bought four children's books by the same author. One was a UK edition and cost around £6. The other three were US editions and cost under £3 each. They took four days longer to arrive – but I was warned about the delay when ordering and was quite happy with it.

SHOPPING SITES AND COMPARISONS

Many portal sites have shopping sections, and you will now find an increasing number of sites dedicated to supporting shopping. The advantage of using one of these sites rather than going directly to the shops is that you can get information on different retailers before plunging into a particular shop. Some sites also offer product comparisons, enabling you to enter the product you want and get a direct comparison of prices and availability from the different retailers.

A special class of sites offer products where prices are reduced using mass buying power, or last minute purchasing. You will also find sites providing auction sales – either of new products or selling items input by other individuals – and personal sales sites. An auction adds a whole new sense of excitement to the buying process, but make sure you understand just who is responsible for making sure you get your money's worth if the retailer or auction house is only acting as a channel between you and the vendor.

Sample Sites

Shopping sites and comparisons

Try these examples, or look in any of the major search engines and portals for their shopping section.

UK

- Bookbrain (book comparison site) – www.bookbrain.co.uk
- Ezoka (mass buying power) – www.ezoka.com
- Indigo Square (Barclaycard mall) – www.indigosquare.com
- Pricerunner (advertised price comparison) – www.pricerunner.com
- QXL (auctions) – www.qxl.com
- Shopsmart (general shopping and comparisons) – www.shopsmart.com

US

- Buyer's Index (product search) – www.buyersindex.com
- Catalog City (general shopping) – www.catalogcity.com
- Comparison Shop (comparisons) – www.comparisonshop.com
- Ebay (auctions) – www.ebay.com

THEY MIGHT BE GLOBAL – BUT YOU AREN'T

It's great being able to buy something special from a different part of the world, but remember that the ease with which you cross the globe isn't

Welcome to BookBrain.co.uk
The smartest way to buy books on the web...

BookBrain.CO.UK

Search for [   ] in [Title ▸] 🔍

Instant Stress Management, Bring Calm to Your Life Now *Clegg, Brian*

Publisher	Kogan Page
Publication Date	1/1/2000
Binding	Paperback
ISBN	0749431164
List Price £	9.99
Description	The book comprises around 70 exercises, each taking between five and twenty minutes, which can be used to control stress.

BookBrain has searched **14** On-Line Booksellers, it was found at the **13** listed. Bookshops are listed in Total Price(inc. p&p) order. Click the bookshop name to be taken to their site, where you can buy.

Available from our Premier Sponsor : WHSmith Online

WHSmith online	Notes	Availability	Price	Delivery	Total
	Shipping £2.24 + 50p per item, max £15.	Normally 1 - 2 Days	6.99	2.74	9.73

Bookshop	Notes	Availability	Price	Delivery	Total
Swotbooks	Shipping £2.40 per order, free above £50	Stock Item	6.89	2.40	9.29
Alphabetstreet	Free shipping	Usually ships in 24 hours	9.49	0.00	9.49
Internet Bookshop	Shipping £2.24 + 50p per item, max £15.	Normally available for dispatch within 48 hours	6.99	2.74	9.73

Figure 10.2 A book shopping comparison site (Bookbrain)

necessarily going to apply to the products you buy. Keep an eye on shipping charges. While it's quite possible that you can find something at a bargain price compared with your local shops, you will have to pay to get it here, and the further it comes, the more it might cost and the longer it might take. Responsible Web shops give an idea of the time taken to ship – if you can't find the information, drop them an e-mail to query it.

Remember too that by buying abroad you aren't necessarily exempt from local taxation. You may need to pay import duty on objects bought from abroad. Finally, watch out for different technical standards. This isn't just a matter of making sure an electrical product works with the local mains voltage. The United States and Europe, for example, have different video standards – you can't play a US video on a European video recorder and vice versa. Similarly, DVDs, the compact movie video disks, have an area code which may prevent them from playing in a different part of the world. Computer software presents a more subtle distinction. It is often 'localized', turning the US original into your local language (even UK English versions are different). Software bought abroad may well run, but might have subtle differences.

SOFTWARE FROM THE WEB

A particularly attractive product to buy from the Web is software. Subject to the provisos in the next paragraph, there is no waiting for shipping, no need to move from your desk – you can pay your money and download immediately. In fact, if the product is shareware, you don't even have to pay straight away, you can try before you buy (which for many quick applications of a utility might be all you ever need).

It sounds gloriously simple, and it is, up to a point. Bear in mind, though, that modern software can be quite big. You are never going to download a CD-based adventure game (one of my favourites occupies 3 gigabytes, which would literally take weeks to download via a modem). Even a serious business package can be a chunky 200 megabytes. However, you will find plenty of software, particularly utilities, in the 1–10 megabyte range, which is perfectly capable of being downloaded.

Once you've got your software you ought to back it up – otherwise, one glitch on your hard disk and you have lost your investment. A second proviso is that you will have to manage without paper manuals. I like something I can have on my desk to consult – but buying over the wire precludes this, unless you are prepared to print out a disk-based manual. Finally, there is the risk of virus infection. From a reliable supplier this isn't a high risk, but it is always there; if you intend to download software from the Web you ought to invest in virus protection software.

Computer viruses

zoom in

Viruses are malignant software, designed to do something unexpected, which might range from putting up a silly message to deleting everything on your hard disk. The two main sources of viruses are word processor documents and programs you run. If you download either of these from the Web, it's a good idea to have virus-checking software on your PC, and regularly update it, as new viruses appear all the time.

If you are downloading a document, modern word processor software usually has an option not to run macros (little programs built into the document), which are the only way a virus can be transmitted with a document. Programs can be more sneaky – remember, for example, that not only can the program you buy be infected, but also the setup program that you get to install it.

All the big names in virus checkers have Web sites where you can find out more. See:

- McAfee (US) – www.mcafee.com
- Norton (US) – www.symantec.com
- Sophos (UK) – www.sophos.com
- Trend Micro (US) – www.antivirus.com

Buying software directly from the Web may sound hazardous, but remember that you can get what you want when you buy it this way – especially useful if you are under pressure and receive a document that needs a special program to read it, or you need a product to develop a presentation for tomorrow. If you take a sensible approach to buying software online (which includes having a virus checker), it makes a lot of sense.

Sample Sites

Software shopping

Plenty of software publishers sell direct, as do third parties. This is only a small subset of the available sources – use a search engine to find more. Some of the sites on this list aren't vendors, but provide pointers to other sites where software is available:

- Freeware – www.freewareweb.com
- Jungle Download Shop – jungle.bayonet.com
- Lotus – www.lotus.com
- Microsoft – www.microsoft.com
- Netscape – www.netscape.com
- Shareware.com – www.shareware.com
- UK shareware – www.ukshareware.com
- ZDNet Downloads – www.zdnet.com/downloads

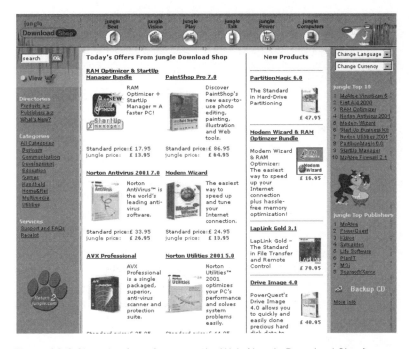

Figure 10.3 Shopping for software on the Web (Jungle Download Shop)

11 SKILLS
Getting launched

- A quick reminder;
- Start to use it.

PULLING IT TOGETHER

By now you should have developed some essential skills for mining information from the Internet – if you haven't, go back and try some of the exercises. It is impossible to overemphasize the importance of practice to good use of the Internet for getting hold of information. A couple of evenings spent trying out various techniques on a wide range of subjects will stand you in good stead when you need something urgently.

This chapter is, in effect, a super recap, pulling together the key aspects of the process. It may be that you know it all now, in which case you can ignore it – otherwise, it's a useful reminder to keep the key points of getting the best out of the Internet in front of you.

KNOW WHAT YOU WANT

Although it's great fun to browse around the Web, simply enjoying the stream of multimedia and entertainment, it isn't a practical way to get to particular information, or to research a topic. In fact, if you want anything more than a simple fact, the best approach is to start by taking a step back from the computer and establishing just what it is that you are looking for. This doesn't have to take long. Just spend a few moments thinking over what you are interested in and jotting down the prime keywords to use in your search.

SEARCH SMART

Make use of the different search engines' capabilities and the wider facilities to extend the search to many engines. Don't stick to the simple search terms, but be prepared to wade in with more advanced forms if necessary. It's a good idea to practise with these until they become habitual – the most complicated thing about Boolean searching is the name once you've had a bit of practice. And remember that search engines aren't all there is to mining information from the Internet, with everything from indexes and newsgroups to expert sites and Web rings available.

FILTER AND REFINE

You have to be immensely lucky to hit the exact information you want in the first few responses from a search. Use the techniques discussed in this book to filter down huge lists of hits, to refine a search in a particular direction, or to take a tangential leap suggested by one of the initial pages returned. This needn't be a long process. With practice, it can be achieved almost as quickly as the initial search.

HIT THE TARGET...

Get what you want and get out. The Internet is great for browsing around when you've got nothing better to do, but don't let it become a problem when you want to get on. Make sure you bookmark the most relevant pages so you can return to them immediately. Depending on what you intend to do with the result, consider copying into a word processor, or printing off.

... BUT BE PREPARED TO GIVE UP

It saves a lot of frustration if you remember that, while the Internet may be the biggest free(ish) collection of information in the world, it isn't complete. You will sometimes fail when looking for something on the Internet. This doesn't mean that you should give up when you hit the first hurdle, but some targets will elude you. When this occurs, it's time to go elsewhere (and quite probably pay through the nose). You might even consider stepping into your local library or bookshop. Like all convenience stores, the Internet has its drawbacks that sometimes make it the wrong place to go.

But don't let the doom mongers who interpret this as an indication that the Internet is useless for research depress you. That is absolute garbage. For all of us who don't class ourselves as professional researchers, and for many who do, there has never been such a superb resource, readily available from your desktop. Don't knock it.

GO FORTH AND START MINING

The fact that you've read this book (and stuck doggedly to the last paragraph) shows that you probably want something out of the Internet. In fact, you are likely to increasingly depend on it. There remains nothing else but to get to the keyboard and start mining for information. Good luck.

APPENDIX
Getting on to the Internet

- Getting connected;
- Hardware;
- Software.

WHERE TO START

If you're already hooked up to the Internet, you can ignore this appendix. It's for those poor unfortunates who haven't yet got the connection. The bad news is that electronic communications is a complex field, laden with jargon. The good news is that you don't need to know too much about it. This appendix is a quick guide to getting on to the Internet.

USING SOMEONE ELSE'S

If you are starting from scratch, it's not a bad move to get a feel for what it's all about by using someone else's connection to the Internet. This might be a friend's equipment, the facilities at work or a cyber-café. Each option has its attractions and problems. A friend will probably give you some handholding, but unless you are prepared to pay their bills might not be too enthusiastic about you spending hours online. Many business connections to the Internet are restricted and can only be used for work purposes. Cyber-cafés can work out quite expensive, though they're good for a quick dip into the online world.

Bear in mind, also, that speeds vary wildly depending on both how you connect to the Internet and the facilities at the site you are trying to access. A cyber-café, for example, will usually have much faster connections than you might have at home. Don't build up unreasonable expectations if this is your first taster of the online world. Even with a fast connection, the information you are trying to get your hands on could be on a slow machine, or might be very popular, bringing everything down to a crawl. Using the Web as a resource requires a degree of patience.

SOMETHING TO LOOK AT

It may seem obvious, but you can't get access to the Internet by a wire straight into the head (yet). You need something at your end to look at and interact with. Far and above the most popular way of getting into the Internet is through PCs (personal computers). Increasingly there are other options, such as set-top boxes for digital TV. Generally the PC approach will be the most flexible, while set-top boxes will typically give a faster response but may only allow you access to a fraction of the content of the Web, with very limited interaction.

It's bad enough looking at how to connect to the Internet without worrying about how to choose a PC as well. Whether you buy a new PC or use an existing one is up to you. As long as it is capable of handling graphics (typically a Windows PC or an Apple Macintosh) you should be okay. Most speed problems with Internet access come from the connection, not the PC – but it would be a good idea to have a fair amount of free disk space (200–300 Mb, perhaps), as it is very useful to have space to keep the efforts of your Web trawling to look at later. The only proviso is that PCs that predate the late 1990s may not have a USB port, the high speed link that many external communication devices use.

MODEMS, ISDN AND OTHER HARD WORDS

So you've got your PC – just pop in a disk and go? Maybe. You will need a box to sit between your PC and the socket on the wall. If you are lucky, your PC will come with one built-in – many modern ones do – but you need to check. Most of us still connect to the Internet through phone lines. These come in two basic forms: analogue (the sort of phone line that everyone had until recently) and digital, often known by the suitably imposing sounding initials ISDN.

This analogue or digital business is nothing to do with being connected to a digital exchange. Most telephone exchanges are now digital, offering services like caller identification and ring back, but the line to your home is more likely to be analogue – assume it is unless you have reason to believe otherwise.

Analogue lines connect to the Internet using a box called a modem. This can be a separate box that sits alongside your PC, or a board that you stick inside. The separate boxes (external) have the advantages of being easier to fit – you generally just plug them in the back of the PC – and they often have a few extra features. Modems on a PC board (internal) have the advantages of being slightly cheaper, don't require a separate plug to power them and don't get in the way. Although we are only interested here in a modem as a way of connecting to the Internet, practically all modems also act as faxes. Some more sophisticated (and more expensive) devices also act as answering machines, and some will even continue to provide fax and answering facilities when the PC is switched off.

Once your modem is fitted, your PC will need to be able to connect to it. If you are using a PC with Windows 95 or above and it is a modern modem, it should be detected by the Plug and Play system with very little extra action. You may need to put in a disk supplied with the modem – check your instructions for details.

If you have an ISDN line, don't rush out and get a modem – it won't work. Instead you need an ISDN terminal adapter, which might work differently at a technical level, but is still just a box that sits between your PC and the socket. ISDN comes in a number of flavours – most recently in a sort of combo package that can be used as ISDN or analogue lines. It is worth saying that setting up an ISDN connection can be considerably more fiddly than a modem. If you aren't sure of what you are doing with ISDN, make sure you have a good support agreement.

The latest generation of connection equipment makes even ISDN seem to operate at a snail's pace. Products like cable modems (not really modems at all) and ADSL offer hugely faster connection speeds. Usually this comes at a price – but for serious users it is worthwhile. One consideration with these high speed links is that they are usually always on – you don't have to dial up to get a connection. The good news about this is you can have constant information flows to your PC. The bad news is that your PC is open to attack from Internet hackers, and an always-on connection should be accompanied by appropriate software protection: check with your vendor.

DOES SPEED MATTER?

It certainly does. This isn't a matter of boy racer go-faster stripes; speed of connection is the inverse of waiting time. The faster you connect, the less you have to wait. This is good both because it saves you getting frustrated, and reduces your phone bills (or equivalent). Of course (like everything else in this business) it isn't quite as simple as it seems. As I've already mentioned, the limit on speed could be the information you are trying to get to rather than your connection, but generally speed matters.

Connection is measured in the rather inflated currency of bits per second. Modern modems will run at up to 56,000 bits per second (though more likely to be around 44,000 – the speed a modem runs is dependent on the quality of the line). To put this in context, a single letter is 8 bits, while a web page might be anything from 30,000 bits up to millions and millions – the more text (and particularly the more pictures), the bigger it is.

Switching to ISDN gives a speed hike to 64,000 bits per second – and added reliably too. Where a modem's communication rate will slow down significantly if there any buzzes and clicks on the line, ISDN doesn't have any glitches. What's more, you will normally have two ISDN lines you can link together (at twice the connection charge), doubling throughput. Fancy connections like cable modem, ADSL and ATM (yet more initials we won't even bother to discuss) push rates up over the 1 million bits per second mark, at least when it's coming towards you. Such systems are generally 'asymmetric', being slower to send information back – but most Web communications are biased this way too.

GETTING CONNECTED

So you've got your PC, you've got your box – you just connect up, right? Sorry – the Internet isn't a place: you can't ring it up. You need to connect up to someone else's computer that is permanently part of the Internet. Luckily there are plenty of such people who are happy to give you a link to the Internet, for a price. These so-called ISPs (Internet service providers) are the final link in the chain.

Broadly ISPs fall into two camps. There are the multinational big names – like AOL, MSN and CompuServe – and local ISPs. Big names are safe, but stolid. They will often provide you with fewer Internet facilities, but will balance this by providing their own proprietary content, which only their members can access. Local ISPs are often better value for money as pure Internet access, but may give less support and be more fiddly to connect to. Try to find a comparative review in a PC magazine to get a feel for the current market.

Watch out for different pricing plans. On top of your phone bill, you may be charged by your ISP. Some are free, depending on advertising or a rake-off from the phone bill; some use a flat fee; others charge by the hour, or have a mixture. Depending on how you will use your connection, you need to consider these options very carefully. Increasingly, it is possible to connect to the Internet with no phone charges, or a fixed, small amount for connection. Consider these schemes if you are a heavy user (usually there is a monthly subscription to pay), but check the small print to make sure that you can stay connected as long as you want to, and that you won't be penalized for heavy use.

Once you have selected your ISP, you will generally be provided with a disk to install software. Once this is on your PC, you should be able to connect up at last. The minimum an ISP should provide you with is the ability to see the World Wide Web, access to Internet newsgroups and an e-mail address. Others will give you multiple e-mail addresses, your own Web space, proprietary Web sites and various other facilities.

SOFTWARE

Your ISP will generally provide you with software. The Internet is a rare world where much of the software you need is free. You will definitely need a Web browser and an e-mail package. You may also want a newsgroup reader and other software.

The Web browser is your window on to the World Wide Web. It is the program you run to look at Web information. Both major contenders – Microsoft's Internet Explorer and Netscape's Navigator – are good, and both are free. E-mail software comes bundled with either – there's no need to splash out here to get started.

YOUR OWN SITE

Although it's fairly peripheral to using the Internet for reference, you may wish to set up your own Web site to publish information to the world. It's quite an exciting prospect (provided anyone ever finds your site). A good starting point is the free space many ISPs bundle with their connection. They will often also provide free or cheap software for putting together a Web site – if they don't there is plenty of good software available at reasonable prices. A modern Web site editor is not unlike a word processor – quite easy to pick up.

If you take your Web site seriously, you will want to move away from the ISP at some point. By using a professional Web host you can have your own 'domain name' – a personalized Web address. So instead of being members.aol.com/blooper you can be www.blooper.com – as long as someone else hasn't got that address first. Professional Web sites are also faster for your readers to access and usually get better coverage by search engines. If you decide to go this way it's probably best to take professional advice on a good host: the business is a minefield.

Index